Wearing combovers

and 49 other Things That the Modern Man Shouldn't Do

Wearing combovers

and 49 other Things That the Modern Man Shouldn't Do

carl walker

ROBERT HALE • LONDON

Introduction

How many great ideas started from a drunken conversation in a pub? In all honesty I can't provide a definitive answer to that question, but I don't suspect there are too many. I very much doubt that Darwin formulated the theory of evolution while lagered-up at his local tavern. That between visits to the outhouse to spray barely processed high-strength ale down his trousers he realized that the origin of species could be accounted for by the force of natural selection on congenital characteristics. And I doubt that a plastered Thomas Edison was asking someone what he was doing looking at his bird when he realized that carbonized bamboo filaments could act as effective light bulbs.

It is at this juncture that I want to separate myself from the great thinkers in history (not a challenging thing for me to do) by saying that my idea for this book was generated in a drunken conversation in a pub between myself and two friends. For a reason that escapes me, we were trying ham-fistedly to discern which kind of men couldn't be trusted and why. By this I don't mean which particular men. There was a chap in our local pub at the time who told me on more than one occasion that he was going to kill me if I beat him at pool. Apart from making me play pool like Stephen Hawking (without the computer), this generated a very reasonable sense of distrust on my part. However, I doubt that many readers would be particularly engaged in the story of Colin from the pub. No, what we meant was particular *types* of men.

We knew that we couldn't trust men whose arms didn't swing when they walked. We knew that we couldn't trust men who played the bongos (or at least referred to them as a musical instrument), or men who wore ties with comedy cartoon characters on them, but we didn't know why. So I did a little research and found that others also had types of people that they didn't trust. These ranged from John Wayne's failure to trust men who didn't drink to an unknown source claiming not to trust any man who, when left alone with a tea cosy, didn't put it on his head. Reading these, I quite quickly realized two things. Firstly, and most disappointingly, if left alone, I would put a tea cosy on my head. Secondly, there was a group of men that I knew couldn't be trusted, but didn't always know why. I mean, I found it very easy to account for why you shouldn't trust a man who is a pushy father or a man who designs the barbs at the top of security fences, but ask me to account for why I couldn't trust men who didn't like watching television or men who rode fold-up bikes and I was stumped. These guys were going to require some thought and research.

Moreover, it became obvious as I selected the types of men for this book that various friends identified with these types to a greater or lesser degree. Indeed, an Irish friend who shall remain nameless seemed to fall into every category. So, to save Geoff McGimpsey's feelings, I knew we needed a new angle.

What started out as a way to try to account for types of men you can't trust became something different as I realized trust wasn't always the problem. So I thought about these fifty men and what they had in common and, suddenly, like Archimedes in the bath, I had my eureka moment. I knew what it was. I realized that it wasn't necessarily that you didn't trust these men, but that there was not a single one that you wanted to spend any time with. Basically, you didn't want to sit facing them at the Christmas dinner table. They were the kinds of guys that would make you pine for your no-longer-quite-so-on-the-ball granny to come back to the table and spend some more time talking in great detail about her sex life while her false teeth fell into her ample tumbler of sherry. Yup, I had it. These were men you simply didn't like.

However, I still felt a little uneasy. I still had a nagging feeling that there was more to these guys than my just not liking them. It wasn't that simple and it probably wasn't enough to entertain the discerning reader. Giving you a list of fifty people I don't like is about as interesting and informative as giving you a run-down of what my last fifty visits to the toilet looked like (which no one should have). Moreover, this approach was going to make me feel like that guy in every group who responds to a night out at a comedy club by suddenly trying to talk to friends like a comedian in the pub afterwards. The one who thinks that their own peculiar brand of observational comedy will hit the mark and starts numerous sentences with the preamble, 'Don't you hate it when...', all the while proving that there is a reason he is fixing photocopiers rather than doing stand-up.

No, this needed to be more. It needed be of use to people. So eventually it became a book about the more eccentric characteristics of the western male, a kind of idiot's guide to the male species. Men are odd. They do odd things that you don't find women doing. They do things that they shouldn't do. We hear loads of nonsense about not understanding the fairer sex, but how often do you see a woman cycling with no hands, or throwing sweets up and catching them in her mouth in public? How often do you see women carrying bunches of keys so big that they can't walk straight, or wearing comedy socks? How often do you see a woman juggling, or jumping over gates that she can easily walk through?

Make no mistake, dear reader: men are the oddballs, and I hope this book goes some way to explaining why. So here it is, a chance to have a gentle laugh at the foibles of the modern western male: *Wearing Combovers and Forty-Nine Other Things That the Modern Man Shouldn't Do*.

Don't wear a combover

Now, losing your hair in itself is not necessarily a grave problem. You are not going to be given six months to live just because you have gone a little Jack Nicholson at the sides. But your reaction to balding? Well, that is absolutely key. Everyone more or less goes through the following stages of balding:

Stage one: You notice it looks a little thinner on top. However, for generations your family has been a bastion of full-headed stallions, so you understandably reason that this can't be baldness. Hell, your genes are too good for this bullshit. Besides, you have your mother's hair, everyone says so. Rule baldness out immediately. No problem. Hairdresser probably just thinned it a little bit too much. Make mental note not to go back to that bloke. What a hatchet job. Might write a 'you made me look like that guy from *Star Trek*' letter of complaint. Probably think better of it.

Stage two: For a prolonged period of time you will hang in a strange 'am I?/aren't I?' limbo. Depending on your mood you will either be receding or paranoid. Other people won't have noticed yet. If there are any hairdos you have always wanted but never tried then now is the time. Make no mistake, if you are thinking like this then nature already has you on the stopwatch. You look more closely at your family tree and realize that almost everyone, on both sides of the family, women included, had a head like the Millennium Dome by the time they were thirty. Damn, how could you not have noticed?

Stage three: You are still not yet ready to use the 'B' word. Instead, 'thinning' and 'receding' are much better. These more accurately represent a man who still has more hair than pate. At this stage you still consider yourself to be categorically different from fully bald people and will probably make jokes about them to ram home the point. Only the other people around you will understand this as a sign of projective anxiety from a man whose brain sits under a rapidly balding forehead. You are prone to getting tetchy if anyone insinuates that you are on a one-way freeway to looking like the end of a roll-on deodorant. As far as you are concerned it's still all under control. Nothing to see here people, move along.

Stage four: Wake up one day and think, 'Shit, when did that happen?' You went to bed looking like Bruce Willis circa *Moonlighting* and woke up looking like a condom that has split at the end. Of course, the transition didn't actually happen overnight; your various attempts at hair management simply haven't allowed you to acknowledge the changes.

Stage five: It looks like you're probably going bald, so you shave it off, just in case. You focus your energies on not being bald before your mates are. This will be the consolation prize now that inevitability has finally shaken admission into you. You are in a race with (hopefully male) friends. You now start to take as much interest in their hairlines as your own. As a result, you laugh especially loudly when someone makes a joke about balding friends' domes as long as yours sails under the radar. You won't have this luxury for long, so make the most of it. You wear hats a lot. If someone asks if this is to cover up your pate you tell them you have always worn hats. And to fuck off, since you are still a bit tetchy at this juncture. You might experiment with a bandanna at times. Words cannot fully convey just what a bad idea this is. At best you are going to look like a pirate who has been kicked off his ship for trying to hump the ship's dog; at worst you will look like a bald man trying to hide his balding head with a bandanna.

Stage six: You grow your hair back one last time, just to double check. You try to fashion your new balding dome into the same hairdo you had when you weren't bald. This doesn't work, so you try instead to cover as much of your head as possible. You look eighty-five. Then you try to grow the bits at the sides long to see if that helps. Now you look like an eighty-five-year-old sex pest. OK, you were right the first time.

Stage seven: OK, fuck it, you're bald. Console yourself with some obviously false and trite truisms about bald men, including their being more virile, more attractive to the opposite sex, and more able to coax a few extra inches out of their penises through the medium of mime. These are (sadly) not true.

Once through the above stages there are, to my mind, three ways to react to becoming a chrome-dome and, as an act of sacrilege to the memory of Sergio Leone, I will label them the good, the bad and the ugly.

There is only one good way to go bald and it doesn't require NASA to figure it out. Three words: shave it off. There are no ifs and no buts. You cannot be bald with any variant of long hair without looking like a nudist from the 1970s. And that's the absolute best you can hope for. Vin Diesel, Patrick Stewart, Michael Stipe, Bruce Willis, Andre Agassi (eventually) and Ross Kemp have figured this out and, as a result, are paragons of the good way to be a bald man. Of course, their continued success in their respective disciplines was not dependent on this decision. Michael Stipe would still have written 'Everybody Hurts' and 'The One I Love' if he had looked like a skinny Donald Trump and Andre Agassi would still have won all four tennis Grand Slams if he had a bald head with long hair at the back, drawn into a greasy ponytail. But the bottom line is: you have to shave it off. Self-respect demands it. You cannot wear and style something that isn't there. It's over. Accept it. Move on. And people will like you more for it.

Now we come on to the bad. The bad is bad, but bear in mind that it is not as bad as the ugly. The bad constitutes men who have gone or are going bald and take up one of the numerous artificial options available to allow them to hang on to their hair. Step up William Shatner, Burt Reynolds and Elton John. The problem with this option is twofold. Firstly, it signals a degree of enfeebling vanity that will forever mar any sense of personal integrity or credibility. It is just not possible to take a man who is utilizing a hair technology seriously. He could be telling you your tests suggest it might be cancer and your mind would still be dominated by the thought that this man looks like a tool. Secondly, these artificial options always, always, always look shit.

Wigs are the hair technology for those who don't have the financial resources to purchase more advanced hair technologies and are a perfect foil for the receding head, barring the tiny detail that the join between the wig and the natural hair has all the subtlety of a row of arseholes sewn around the circumference of your head.

Those who are prepared to invest a little more in their hair duplicity can go for hair transplant surgery, the most famous proponents of which are Elton John and Wayne Rooney. This involves transplanting plugs of skin from areas of the scalp that still have hair to those that don't. The only drawback with this is that, despite our ability to split the atom, put a man on the moon and grow ears on the backs of mice (bet they don't get caught by cats sneaking up to them), a man with all the money in the world still can't get hair surgery that looks any better than as if he has drunkenly stumbled into a ladder holding a tub full of pubes and glue.

And, finally, we have the 'third way' of baldness, what we might call the 'ugly', by way of completing this shaky analogy. This is the combover. One of the great public exhibits of combover art, for art it surely is, is the American business entrepreneur, Donald Trump. For the tiny minority of you out there yet to be fully acquainted with the modern combover, it is a hairstyle worn only by the prince of bald men, the man whose vanity and powers of self-denial are beyond reach. A combover is where a man grows the hair on one side of his head (and I mean side, not side of the top) inordinately long, perhaps a foot long (although they have been spotted up to five feet long), and sweeps it all the way over his head to the other ear in such a fashion that the man magically becomes no longer bald. Problem solved. At least it is in a world consisting wholly of blind people, simpletons and blind simpletons.

Joking aside, the principal problem with Mr Combover is that he has made the assumption that the people who share his planet are drooling remedials whose ability to talk and breathe at the same time should qualify them for Mensa. What is a man doing when he summons a combover from the depths of Hades? He is using it to hide his bald head. Now he's not hiding it from children à la hide-and-seek. It's not a party game for kids where they have to guess who in the room went bald when he was twelve. Nope, he's hiding it from *us*. You and me. Adults. Ergo, by definition, he thinks we can't see it. He has carried out the hair equivalent of gluing tusks onto a frog and calling it an elephant and we are supposed to buy it. A common defence of those sporting the combover is that they always combed their hair that way, even before they began to go bald. The shrewdest of minds can, however, counter this by noting that a normal side parting tends not to have its genesis so low down that it looks like it has been scraped up directly from the wearer's back passage.

I genuinely worry about the motivation of any man who goes to such extreme lengths, for so long, to maintain a combover because, make no mistake, a combover is a twenty-four hours a day, seven days a week, job. It is not for those of a capricious nature. You don't get bank holidays and Christmas off. Having to deal with a combover is literally a full-time position. As such, these guys are usually doing two full-time jobs: your standard 37.5 hours a week in the office or factory and double that managing the dead rat on their heads. If they let the veneer down, even for one single day, they cannot go back. Combovers do not set themselves. These guys don't just wake up, look in the mirror and find that a gravity-defying clump of hair has migrated from one side of their head to sit on the other out of the goodness of its heart. A combover is not a haircut, it is a battleground, and it is not a battleground for the meek. You think air-traffic controllers have stressful jobs? Those guys don't know they are born. I'll give you real stress: the constant vigilance of the combover, that's stress. Next time you see a combover, watch how much time its wearer spends scraping what is left of his hair into position, like a demented heroin addict clawing for skag in a clump of straw.

In this war, gravity is not their only foe, either. The wind is an arch enemy, the veritable sniper in the undergrowth. A single, misplaced gust can blow the combover back to its source, leaving its wearer looking like a man who had to evacuate the hairdresser's at a particularly critical point in the haircut following a fire alarm. And that can happen at any time, at the click of a finger. Years of this constant war with gravity and wind will eventually take their toll, make no mistake. Mr Combover has the 1,000-yard stare of any seasoned combat veteran, a hardy look generated by years of battle with the elements.

Don't wear a ponytail that never comes out

If, for the duration of your life, it has been your unbending wish to look like a cross between one of the bad guys from *Miami Vice* (who gets killed early) and a man whose sole desire is to collect vintage coins, then don't let me stop you. If this is the case, however, do yourself a favour and at least let the ponytail out to roam free every now and again.

Don't ignore the golden rules when it comes to dogs

Dog rule one: Don't say, 'Don't worry, he won't bite'

Picture the scene: you are walking in a park and from out of nowhere you hear a voice shout, 'Don't worry, he won't bite,' as a dog flies towards you, salivating and growling. Well actually, my friend, the evidence is telling me something quite different. Let's get this straight. You have a creature bounding towards you that could conceivably do you some very serious damage and yet you are supposed to trust a complete stranger who tells you not to worry. Pray tell, on exactly what grounds should you trust this man? He expects you to put your life, face and livelihood in his hands for what reason?

The crux of this problem is that I resent these people for asking for what is essentially a social contract in such a way that I, frankly, have little option but to accede. My only options are to run away (which I understand encourages some creatures even more), attack the creature (socially unacceptable) or remain still, effecting a veneer of icy calm in the face of the onslaught. I don't like any of these options, but nor should I have to. I resent this too. I did not come to the park to play chicken with an unknown dog, just like I don't cross the road to play chicken with the traffic. What is the difference between this and being chased by a car when you cross the road and hearing a loudspeaker saying, 'Don't worry, he always brakes'?

You can't run from a dog because, apart from anything else, you will look like a yellow-bellied figure of fun. If you do this children will laugh at you. This is not fair. Some people yell at other people's dogs and I have seen the owners get cross with this. If you attack the dog you are breaking an entrenched social norm and could take a kicking from an angry owner. All of a sudden you become the bad guy. Besides, if, like me, you would struggle in a wrestling match with a Chuckle brother, this is not really an option anyway. So you are forced into this icy calm veneer – perhaps with a cheeky smile or a friendly exhortation or welcome for the dog – whilst everything inside you is shouting, 'Cover your balls'. I mean everything. It is obviously not practical to spend a lifetime immediately covering your balls every time you see a dog. Or covering them whilst doing that manifestly effeminate wince where you turn away and lift one leg up. These are not cool things to do. Apart from the greater challenge of reminding you of your mortality, they make you look like a real, one hundred per cent, bona-fide coward. So you have to take on the challenge of playing it cool and hoping the thing doesn't make a bee-line for your nether regions. What prize for the ice-cool hero who chases a dog but has his plums in its mouth? Not for me, thanks. I can't be the only one who has found himself considering which parts of his anatomy he should cover as the creature bounds towards him. I only have two arms; do I use one to cover my groin and the other to cover my face (at such an angle that it might cover my neck too)? Perhaps I should offer it the arm I don't use much as a little 'softener', and hope that it takes the bait and leaves the more precious and useful parts of my body intact. I am being forced to play Russian roulette with my own body parts when I only came out for a little bit of fresh air. This is absurd.

You see, as far as I am concerned it is a civil right in the twenty-first century not to be scared that an animal will tear into me in a public place. This may appear old-fashioned, and I apologize if this is the case. Perhaps I am out of step with the current zeitgeist. Maybe nowadays it has been decided that public spaces need a little frisson to keep us all on edge. I am sorry if I have missed this memo. I simply can't believe that in the time of iPods, space travel and the internet, intelligent people have to run away from dogs at their local park.

That this man is prepared to put you in this dilemma without a moment's consideration is fundamentally unfair and selfish. He is asking for a social contract, knowing full well that you have no choice. He scares you, makes you feel uneasy, and proves that he has no self-respect and hardly ever apologizes. This beast has almost trotted off with a bellyful of Walkerballs and the owner does not even have the courtesy to say sorry. He thinks that an apology is not warranted; after all, it was the dog and not him suddenly acting up.

I swear that, one day, I will walk through the local park with a friend and, as soon as I see one of these men intone that everything is OK as their dog speeds towards some poor unsuspecting soul, I will release my masterplan. I will have an accomplice run towards the dog owner, looking crazed and ferocious, and with a huge machete in his hand. He will run right up to the owner and yell in their face and jump up and down while all the time waving the machete around. I will then jog over (jog, mind, not run), smiling, and say, 'Oh don't worry, he's only playing, he won't hurt you.' I suspect that our dog-owning friend might then understand that IT'S NOT VERY NICE TO SUDDENLY FEEL IN PROFOUND DANGER IN A PUBLIC PLACE.

Dog rule two: Don't own a dangerous dog (and tell people he's actually really sweet)

I was at a public park recently when I chanced upon a man walking an aggrieved-looking pit bull. Every time said dog saw something that it took exception to (which seemed to be most things) it would strain on the leash and bark aggressively. The man would then punch the dog in the face and call it a c***. While this seemed to temporarily cool the dog down I remember thinking two things. The first was that this man might not be the optimal walker of this dog. The second was that repeated punches in the face to an already angry and aggressive dog was not one of the key interventions that I recalled seeing on the *Really Wild Show* when I was a kid. I have also yet to come across any cast-iron research that suggests that screaming the word 'c***' at a dog is likely to yield substantial gains in obedience.

Apparently, in the hands of a responsible owner, a well-trained and well-socialized Rottweiler or pit bull can be a reliable, alert dog and a loving companion. But here we come to the problem. There is a certain type of man who owns violent dogs. Dogs like Rottweilers and pit bulls are responsible for most of the attacks on humans for two, not completely unrelated, reasons:

One: The dogs are temperamentally predisposed to be aggressive.
Two: Very stupid men buy them for this reason.

There are hundreds of different breeds of dog out there offering all sorts of joys to potential owners. Why do some men want a savage, violent little beast that scares the life out of other people? We all know the answer: it's to display their towering masculinity. But why don't they just cut out the middle man and put a baseball bat on a lead and drag it along for a walk? Or, better still, why don't they just take a blown-up photo of their dick out for a walk? At least it won't shit everywhere and they won't have to feed it.

Don't put pictures of you with your children on your Facebook profile page

I have noticed something recently about these new-fangled social-networking sites. It concerns the photographs that some men use to accompany their profiles. It seems to be the case that as soon as many men on these sites have children they literally can't wait to post photos of their little ones as their profile pictures. If they have more than one child they make sure to squeeze as many of the little tykes in as possible. Nothing strange here, I hear you say? After all, surely they are just showing everyone how proud they are of their kids and how important said kids are to their doting father? Pull. The. Other. One.

I can tell the more naïve of readers right now that every single one of these photographs of family bliss and paternal identity is nothing more than an advert for their balls. They scream, 'Hey, everyone who hasn't seen me for ages (and those who have), my balls work. That's right, they work an absolute treat. As do my tubes, my penis and my sperm, which I have absolutely loads of. Loads, do you hear me? So much that I don't even know what to do with it.' They might as well just have a picture of one of their sperm waving hello or moonwalking. Don't try to play us with the cutesie family-man angle gents, that's fine for your grannies, but it doesn't wash with us.

Don't be late, thief

A lack of punctuality is theft. No more, no less. And not the kind of admirably daring theft that secretly impresses people, like bank robbers who make good to Rio with heists of $40 million and have films made about them. No, men who are perpetually late are the equivalent of grubby shoplifters who try to snaffle a can of high-strength lager from their local supermarket just to make sure that they wet the bed that night. Or burglars who get shot in the arse trying to steal the local farmer's telly. Men who are late are stealing our time. Simple as that. Not only are they committing grand larceny, but they are sending you an unambiguous statement which tells you that their time is more precious than yours. It's not hard to be on time.

Don't change your name to one word

Sting and The Edge were, of course, not christened Sting and The Edge. They were christened Gordon Sumner and David Evans. There are numerous accounts of the origins of their nicknames that include bumble-bee jumpers for Sting and standing on the edge of tall buildings for The Edge, but they simply don't wash. Sting and The Edge are called Sting and The Edge because at some point they made the decision that they would like to be called Sting and The Edge. The names 'Sting' and 'The Edge' offered a little bit of vim, a bit of the night, a little bit of crazy and maverick.

However, don't think for a second that this would have been easy for them. Don't write them off as little more than internationally renowned musicians. You have to have two difficult and very unique conversations when you decide to be called The Edge or Sting. First, you have to announce that you are no longer 'David' to a world that might not necessarily be ready to hear that you are no longer 'David':

'Hi, Colin, how's things?'

'Yeah, fine, Dave. How are you?'

'Yeah, good. Thing is though, Colin, I'm not really Dave anymore.'

'Oh. Oh sorry. Is it David now?'

'Well, no, I'm not David either.'

'What do you mean, Dave?'

'I'd like people to call me The Edge from now on.'

'I'm sorry?'

'Yeah, I am now The Edge.'

'Edge of what?'

'Just the fucking Edge, OK? Don't make this any harder than it needs to be.'

'But you're not The Edge, you're David.'

'I fucking am The Edge, see?'

'OK, Dav... er... The Edge, cool.'

(Thirty second pause.)

'Can I ask why?'

'No. The Edge doesn't need to explain why.'

Then, a number of years later, as maturity kicks in, and following morning after morning of screaming 'why' repeatedly in the mirror, they have to make a second change. They realize it's a really, really, really shit name, so then they have to have a second embarrassing conversation:

'Hi, Colin, you OK?'

'Yeah, good thanks, The Edge. How are you?'

'Fine, mate.' (Pause.) 'Listen, would you mind not calling me The Edge anymore?'

'Why not, The Edge? It's what we called you for years.'

'Well, it's just, you know, I'm getting a bit older now, and it feels nice to revert to my family name, you know, with the kids and that.'

(Pause.)

'Well, does this mean you are no longer The Edge or have you lost the edge? I'm confused.'

'No, no, no, I mean, it's just that I quite like Dave.'

'OK, The Ed... er... Dave.'

Don't tell someone you can make a man stop breathing in five seconds

I had a hairdresser who was my regular go-to guy for some time, despite clearly revealing himself to be a lunatic. On one encounter he managed, with quite considerable conversational dexterity, to bring the discussion around to martial arts. He carefully, and in great detail, explained his background in martial arts, almost as if I had walked into the shop and told him that I was the producer of the next Steven Seagal film. He moved from extolling its virtues as a provider of fitness, confidence and self-defence to showing me in very specific detail some of the movements that he could, and would, use to choke a man to death if pushed far enough – he reluctantly confirmed, as if I had pushed him on the topic for half an hour, that he was prepared to kill in the right situation. Any semblance of me being there for a haircut and him being a hairdresser disappeared in a puff of smoke, and one could be forgiven for thinking that I had paid for a sit-down lesson in fucking people up if they try to push you too far. He put the clippers down (my heart sank) and went through a series of mind-bogglingly aggressive and angry manoeuvres that would stop a man from breathing. Always stop them from breathing, mind, never kill them, like this was somehow a temporary state unrelated to death. I was scared, uncomfortable and confused.

He took nearly forty-five minutes to go through his whole Aikido or Tae Kwon Do routine, together with what he would say to his imaginary opponent as he did it (teeth clenched and mumbling things like, 'You don't fucking like that, do you, pal?' or 'Who's in charge now, dickhead?'). I was not going to be the person who put a check on these empowerment fantasies, lest I become the 'pal' in question, so I nodded and tried to manufacture a disinterested interest. To be honest I just wanted to give him my wallet and tell him to take it, that it was all his, that all I wanted was to leave and that I had a young family (I didn't).

Telling other men how good you are at hurting people doesn't work beyond the age of eight (and even then it's touch and go). Don't do it.

Don't swear badly

There are few more powerful signals of a juvenile and socially retarded mind than poor swearing. You may as well walk into a pub in a nappy or phone your dad to ask if you can buy a half of lager. Beginning a swearing apprenticeship in your twenties or thirties is not pretty. However, if you find yourself in such an unfortunate position, don't fret, for I have outlined below some of the classic mistakes that people make when swearing. I have also detailed a few pieces of advice for those who commit such heinous examples of expletive folly.

Remember that swearing, in the right context, is good. And it is cool. When we were young, all and sundry queued up to tell us that smoking was not cool and that we should refrain from it. The problem was that smoking was always cool, it is still cool and it is especially cool if you are a teenager. Well, a similar logic applies to swearing. In the right circumstances and with the right people (e.g. not seven-year-old girls in a church), it is cool. This is important because there is a lobby of anti-swearing disciples who would have us believe that it is one step removed from giving the devil hand relief. I actually believe that, if executed properly, it can be elevated to an art form and, as with all art forms, it has its own Picassos.

So, how do you swear? What are the ground rules, so to speak? Well, I'm going to tell you. At this juncture you might question my authority on the topic. Now, I don't have a particular gift for many things. I will happily admit that my perpetual mediocrity has been a source of mild frustration (only mild) to no end of teachers, family and friends over the years. But I can, with some confidence and conviction, state that I am a very, very good swearer. I don't know why or how. I just am.

Put the swear-words in the right places

This is so central that it hardly needs to be stated. However, you would be amazed by the number of people who entertain the notion that simply dropping the work 'fuck' or 'fucking' into a sentence will lend them the distant cool of an alternative comedian and the sense of intimidating physical presence of a contract killer. It won't. Take the sentence below. Let's say that you are not happy with someone. Who knows, perhaps they have undertaken some kind of behaviour that has transgressed the boundaries of decency and you are amazed that they still have the gall to hang around. You have decided to relay the story to a friend. Without a swear-word it might look something like this:

'I can't believe this guy is still hanging about.'

Of course, this fails to communicate just how cross you are with him for the aforementioned transgression. So you put a swear-word in, because that allows you access to this beautifully rich and expressive set of words that bring alive the sentence that is the representation of your ire. However, you can't do the following:

'I can't believe this guy is still fucking hanging about.'

Putting the swear-word before 'hanging about' suggests that the worst problem here is hanging about, which of course on its own is not a big problem. It doesn't need a swear-word to emphasize it. This does not look good. The listener will immediately know that you don't normally swear and are trying to impress them with a swear-word on this occasion to highlight your tough guy credentials.

'I can't fucking believe this guy is still hanging about.'

This is better, not perfect, but better and highlights that what needs to be conveyed is the degree to which you are unable to comprehend the gall of this man still being there – that you have rarely felt so strongly about a transgression as you do about this. 'Fucking' needs to come before the thing that is the most distressing. Here, it emphasizes that the problem is your incredulity (i.e. the 'fucking' comes before your inability to believe).

However, my own personal preference is:

'I can't believe this fucking guy is still hanging about.'

This is A-grade swearing, especially if you take your time with the word 'fucking', really draw it out and give it emphasis. Here 'fucking' is employed before the guy, to show that he of all the things in the sentence is the most problematic.

Less is more

Less really is more when it comes to swearing. This is the key rule of the successful swearer. You simply cannot get away with ignoring this. You can put a word in the wrong place if your delivery is good, but you cannot get away with too many swear-words. The following sentence does not look good:

'I fucking can't believe this fucking guy is still fucking hanging about.'

You might as well take it to the logical extreme and say the word 'fucking' eight times followed by the word 'c***'. You'll look like an altar boy who has stumbled into a Hell's Angels' bar and is trying to talk his way back out again. And as sure as the Hell's Angels would suss you out, so will others in your conversation. There is no glory to be had in looking like someone whose mum brings his sandwiches to his work when he forgets them. Because this is what you will look like.

Perfect delivery

A swear-word sentence needs perfect delivery. To mumble or trip up over a word in the sentence makes it look like you were concentrating too hard on the swear-word. This makes the whole thing look artificial and self-conscious, and natural swearers don't sound contrived when they swear. Get it right first time or prepare for it to feel like someone has momentarily turned the sound up during *Mr Bean*.

Remember 'fucking' is the most important word in the sentence. By far. Savour it and take a little more time over it than the others. Perhaps count to two in your head as you say it and put some real feeling into it so that the listener is under absolutely no illusion that a) this is the key word in the sentence and b) you are not a happy bunny. That said, don't linger on it for ten minutes or you will look like you are mentally ill.

Don't swear at children

Don't swear at children. That said, if you are in doubt over any of the earlier points on delivery you could do a lot worse than listening to children swear. Yes, that's right, kids. For the hard of thinking out there, not only do most kids over eight swear, but they swear very, very well. I have heard six- or seven-year-olds swear with the breathless control, timing and word place-ment of a soldier in a brothel. Ignore this collective amnesia that represents children as lexical angels who have somehow miraculously managed to avoid the word 'fuck' in the eight years since they were born. They know 'fuck' and 'c***' long before they know what they actually are. As soon as their parents hear them swearing they take the hiding and/or telling-off of a lifetime (if they are lucky) or are told not to be a little c*** (if they are unlucky) and then, and only then, do they know that there is something so very right about swearing.

Don't ignore the barriers to juggling

At some point in their lives men who can't juggle make the decision that they would like to learn to juggle. A number of barriers have to be overcome in order to develop this ability. These have stopped most of us and enabled us to pursue rewarding (or more rewarding) lives, but the juggler flies over these barriers like Colin Jackson.

Thought one: Juggling is clever.
Barrier: No, it isn't. It makes people look like the worst kind of incurable show-off and try-hard, like someone who has no inherent ability to entertain an audience on any level but tries anyway. I always feel a tinge of genuine sadness when I see the look on a juggler's face as he finishes his juggle. It's a look of child-like simplicity and expectancy, a silent plea for hollow praise that makes me feel like I am watching an enfeebled pet that is about to be put down.

Thought two: My time could not be better spent doing anything other than learning to juggle.
Barrier: If you have passed through stage one then this is probably true. If you haven't isolated the fact that juggling isn't clever then you're unlikely to be able to create science and literature of Nobel interest. In fact, you may struggle to use the toilet without a map.

Thought three: I will look good when I am able to juggle.
Barrier: You will look good the way that two dogs rutting looks good, i.e. mildly diverting but ultimately unrewarding (other than for the dogs). Human beings relate to each other in a number of different ways and throwing balls in the air is not one of them. By being a juggler, you have shown that you have spent more time throwing balls in the air than other people have. This should not be advertised.

Thought four: It is a skill that I will be able to use to baffle and amaze viewers for the rest of my life – look at the guys who do it with knives and flaming things.

Barrier: You will never throw knives and flaming things. These people have reached the epoch of juggling aristocracy and whilst I liken it to climbing to the top of a mountain of shit, they deserve a grudging respect for making a living out of throwing things in the air. Even, in the unlikely event that you reach those dizzy heights, I dare someone to stand in front of a professional juggler for more than one minute without having an unbearable urge to shout out, 'Next please.'

Thought five: Let's go!

Barrier: Nothing. You have officially joined the school for the hard of thinking.

On my travels I have encountered a list of the potential benefits that juggling can provide to a wannabe juggler. However, with a little reflection, each has its own problem.

Juggling and learning how to juggle are mentally and physically stimulating.

Not, I repeat not, for this potential juggler. It is as stimulating as a romantic and physically explicit evening with Noel Edmonds.

Juggling is an ideal vehicle for developing the right side of the brain.

Conventional training concentrates on work-related skills, usually logical systems. These are all left-side brain functions. In support of juggling, one juggler optimistically quoted Confucius when he said: 'I hear and I forget. I see and I remember. I do and I understand.' Had Confucius been asked about juggling he would have said, 'I juggle and I bore.'

There are educational benefits to juggling.

Scientists have found that learning to juggle can cause changes in the brain. Using brain scans, the researchers showed that in twelve people who had learnt to juggle, certain brain areas had grown. Parkinson's, Alzheimer's and strokes also cause changes in the brain.

Juggling helps dyslexia.
It has long been thought that juggling can help disabilities such as dyslexia. Personally, I would rather spell like a five-year-old than bore the tits off people by tossing three clubs in the air repeatedly. (I appreciate that this may not be an entirely accurate representation of dyslexia. They spell like four-year-olds.)

Juggling improves physical fitness.
Juggling is a great way to exercise. So is exercise.

Juggling improves eye to hand co-ordination.
Exactly why, in the modern age, do we need eye to hand co-ordination? So that our hand doesn't slip off the mouse? So that we are better at tossing paper into the bin?

Juggling improves ambidexterity.
Another wonderful skill. Most people barely need to use one hand particularly well. Why two? It's about as useful as being able to open your front door using only your butt crack.

Juggling keeps you warm.
Now we are really stretching. So do radiators and clothes.

It is a great confidence-builder.
Apparently it changes your outlook from, 'That's impossible' to 'What's next?' What *is* next? Doing handstands at other people's weddings? Singing a sudden a cappella at a friend's graduation?

It is a genuine aphrodisiac.
I would rather have that evening with Noel Edmonds.

You make new friends.
I would prefer to expand my social circle at a flashers' convention (if, indeed, they convene).

Juggling improves communication.
Now they're just picking words from the dictionary.

It allows you to show off, like a six-year-old tugging at his mother's sleeve.
OK, this one was mine.

Don't leave a high-five hanging

As a cyclist I am often confused about the cycling etiquette of saying hello. For the uninitiated, there is a kind of unwritten code where club cyclists wave or say hello to each other when they pass. This is a rule followed by almost every cyclist and certainly known by all. However, just a few don't play ball. These tend to be the more aloof and superior of the breed; men who view normal cyclists as an insult to their physical pedigree. As a cyclist, this can leave you in a delicate quandary. If you don't say hello then most other cyclists will think you a dick, and they will be right to do so. However, you might end up in the horrific situation of saying hello but being ignored by the intended recipient. And the unreturned cycling hello is like the hanging high-five (a high-five that has not been reciprocated by the intended recipient). It is the most brutal source of minor social shame; like a patch of wet around your groin or being in the wrong place when a passing seagull deposits its lunch. Don't be that man who leaves a high-five hanging and hence forces the high-fiver to quickly and awkwardly put his hand through his hair as if he wasn't even asking for a high-five in the first place. Nobody deserves this.

Don't ride motorbikes

I should admit at this juncture that I am no expert on motorbikes; in fact, far from it. However, I am an expert on idiots and there's an overlap here that lends me some authority when I talk about this topic.

When I was young, a friend of mine at school managed to get hold of a scrambler. For the uninitiated, this is a relatively powerless motorbike used by adolescents and people who can't afford to get good motorbikes. He was playing around on a patch of grass outside his house, so a group of us headed over to his place, eager to check out his new wheels. We all took a go on his bike, going round and round a small hilly field. Of course, it was pretty exhilarating, especially for a group of callow sixteen-year-olds awash with adrenaline, testosterone and the lack of intellectual clarity that is associated with much of the decision-making of male youth. As can be expected, we all went as fast as we could until we fell off. The machine gave us a written invitation to push our boundaries, to find out what it had. Indeed, it also let us show our friends that we were the flesh incarnation of masculinity, a two-legged lion without the tail, big hair and teeth (or propensity to eat people).

All seven of us fell off. And it hurt. It really hurt because it was outrageously heavy. I fell twice. It fell on my right leg both times and it felt like someone had dropped a bag of elephants' arses on my ankle. The falls were inevitable really, not rocket science. What was far less inevitable, and much more interesting, was what happened next. Out of the seven kids, five more or less resolved on the spot not to ride a motorbike again. The other two of our number became long-term motorcycle riders. I was one of the first group. Now, if the wuss police came calling I would gladly go without a fight and enter a 'no contest' plea in the wuss court. Yes, I am a coward, a big, yellow chicken. Shaggy from *Scooby-Doo* would call me a wuss and tell me to get myself together. In fact, in the unlikely event that I landed in an episode of *Scooby-Doo* it would be me comically jumping into Shaggy's arms and shaking at the first sign of the man in the suit chasing us from his haunted hotel. I don't mind this. In fact, if I had the choice between being the guy who jumps into Shaggy's arms in raw fear or the one that Shaggy visits in hospital because he has broken his legs and pelvis on a motorbike (I am aware I am stretching this Shaggy analogy. I don't remember any episodes of *Scooby-Doo* where they visited friends in hospital, unless of course the head doctor put on a monster suit and chased people round the hospital), I know which one I would choose.

While I'll never be able to correct Stephen Fry on an error in his reading of Shakespeare, I am clever enough to realize that THEY ARE DANGEROUS. That's right. We were going at 15 mph and I fell off. It really, really hurt. Twice. And I was struck by the thought that this happened at 15 mph on a (very) light motorbike. I am aware that I have absolutely no idea how to ride a motorbike, then or now, but that's not the point. Such choices present themselves to adolescent males (again, in my experience, most females tend to be smarter and don't become involved in juvenile mechanical pursuits that hurt a lot) and they go one way or the other. You are essentially asked the question, 'Are you a moron or not?' And your answer to that is whether you continue to ride motorbikes or not.

Most motorbike riders have a pathological need to go fast and have a machine which goes frighteningly fast. Hmmm, wonder what the outcome will be? There is no need to pull out the scientific calculators that draw graphs for this conundrum. It's like asking a heroin addict to look after your bag of skag or putting Al Pacino in a film and expecting him not to ruin it by shouting too much. Some things are just going to happen when you put certain circumstances together.

Apparently the United Kingdom has a number of organizations dedicated to improving motorcycle safety by providing advanced rider training. This training is over and above what is necessary to pass the basic motorcycle test. Along with increased personal safety, riders with these advanced qualifications often benefit from reduced insurance costs. Well, I could redesign

those courses in a heartbeat. They need to do just one thing. I would take their money, provide them with a pad and a bit of paper, get them into the room on day one at 9 a.m. and give them a nice cup of tea. Maybe we could do a few icebreakers before kicking things off. Then I would put up my first (and only) PowerPoint slide and it would simply say, in a big font, 'Fucking grow up.' Simple. End of course.

The Carl Walker motorbike achievement awards

So, reader, I am going to leave you with the Carl Walker motorbike achievement awards in recognition of outstanding service in the field of being a bit dim. A special prize of a gold hospital bed, diamond bone pins and a platinum catheter for the winner. In reverse order:

Fourth: the guy that makes a lot of noise without even moving

Yup, these are the guys you see collectively stroking their lengthening penises over the 100 decibel growl of this half-ton metal genital extension outside their houses, looking like rejects from a cross between *Mad Max II* and *Bugsy Malone*. Ask them politely to keep the noise down and they will probably tell you to fuck off. They will accompany this with a raised middle finger in the unlikely event that you misinterpreted their initial invitation. These lads are only a temporary encumbrance since they will be chewing pillow in a local young offenders' institution within six months. Don't be the reason they get sent there.

Third: the touring motorbikers

Ewan McGregor and Charley Boorman are classic examples of this group. Modern day Galahads, they bravely leave their partners at home to bring up their children for months on end whilst this most intrepid of emotional tourists braves the wild dangers of multiple savage landscapes with only millions in the bank should they run into trouble.

Second: the Sunday rider

Ah yes, about 3,000 of them meet every Sunday morning and think that they can drive around in a line of 3,000 whenever and wherever they want. And why shouldn't they? Well, they shouldn't because they make other road users feel nervous. On a Sunday morning the car driver and cyclist get the joy of feeling really pressured by a very long line of frustrated men who desperately want to drive past them so that they, too, can make a lot of noise for twenty yards until they tailgate the next road user. Now I understand that they would like to go out and have a nice, traffic-free jaunt together. There are things I want too. I want Robin Williams to stop making films. I want an act passed in the House of Commons that stops *EastEnders'* characters making big public speeches in the Queen Vic and I want to be able to smoke twenty a day without getting cancer. But I can't. That's life.

First: and now my own personal favourite, yup, it's the man I saw recently flying along ON THE PAVEMENT.

Now, to be fair, it's probably not right to put him in the motorcyclists' category as he was riding what looked like a children's motorbike. This guy was flying along the pavement at about 30 m.p.h. (and without the S&M safety clothing that more responsible riders believe will save their lives; you know, the outfit that is the safety equivalent of riding at 80 m.p.h. in a giant condom). He might as well have flown along with a placard saying, 'I never went to school' on it and, just below, 'Hence I have no rudimentary education'. He is the archetype of his kind. Now most riders would probably disown these people as idiots who are unrepresentative of the clan due to their lack of respect for the rules. But this makes as much sense to me as stalkers having a go at flashers for exposing themselves. This pavement rider is actually an exemplar of the motorcycle mentality, just without all of the paraphernalia that riders use to convince us that they care remotely about their safety. He is a perfect snapshot of the motorbike rider's immortality complex. He is my favourite because he is the most honest motorcyclist on the road (or pavement). He is the man who doesn't care about the safety and convenience of others and can't even be bothered to pretend otherwise.

Don't play late-night snooker in London

Over time I came to realize that, no matter where you lived in London, a visit to your local snooker club would not pass without a group of people beating someone up with snooker cues. The victim always and quite curiously chose to take refuge under the nearest snooker table, which, whilst momentarily providing a degree of safe haven, never felt like a long-term exit plan from what was a moment of coruscating violence. OK, to be fair, I have only visited three snooker clubs in London (in Leytonstone, Lewisham and Croydon, if memory serves me right), but my friend and I were witness to two savage beatings and a fracas which looked like it was about to turn into the third savage beating to bear my witness in a snooker club. What I learned was: if you want to play snooker in London, buy a snooker table.

Don't live with a man who thinks he's Al Pacino in Scarface

When I moved to London, back in the late 1990s, a few things became obvious to me very quickly. I shared a flat in Leytonstone with a student from another university. Said student liked to think of himself as a bit of a 'player'. I knew this because he wore a lot of jewellery that made him look like a simple version of Ali G. He also used to launder drug money for some local small-time goons. This I didn't know. I found out when two men burst through our door one day and asked where the cash card was. I played dumb (to be fair, because I was) while they tore the entire flat to bits from top to bottom.

Throughout this process I made a cup of tea. Wasn't sure what else to do, really, and I thought that if I made it out alive then at least I could tell people about my casual insouciance in the face of life-threatening danger. Life-threatening? But surely you exaggerate, Carl, I hear you say. Well actually, on this rare occasion I am not exaggerating, because said gentlemen rearranging our flat were 'carrying'. That's right, they had guns, or 'pieces,' or 'heat'. As they continued to tear the flat to shreds I went downstairs (to which my new friends seemed not to object) and proceeded to call my girlfriend to ask if she thought I should try to get through my bedroom window and run. It was a very small window and the chance of my man boobs getting caught in the handle was a real possibility so urgent counsel was needed. In the end we thought better of it and the gentlemen found their card and left the flat. I believe they even said goodbye, which really was as much as I could have hoped for. I would have settled for a flesh wound.

Don't run straight ahead if you get chased by a cow

Only recently, a good friend and I were having a stroll up on Devil's Dyke, a popular beauty spot in Sussex. It was a misty, wet day and as we returned to the car we came across a field that we needed to cross. On the way this stretch of land had been clear, but by the time we returned someone had seen fit to drop about fifty huge cows there. I won't lie, this came as a bit of a surprise and, while I was aware that they are generally docile creatures, they still had to be avoided because they were bigger than me and because I am not skilled in the ancient art of spotting a mother protecting her young or differentiating a cow from a bull at distance. However, we had some space, so it felt safe. Or so I thought.

All of a sudden and from nowhere I felt a gentle rumbling behind me and without looking back I knew what was happening. Yes, you've guessed it, a cow was chasing me. I was confused, because like most desk-ridden, housebound twenty-first-century westerners I was unused to being chased by an animal, least of all a big, fat one that should, in principal, only be interested in grass. I scanned my memory and the closest thing to an appropriate solution came in remembering that if a bear chases you the best riposte is to play dead. I briefly flirted with this option, but a quick glance at the by-now angry cow told me that this would not be the optimal way of dealing with this beast. Apart from anything else, my friend was with me and he would have wet himself at both my idiocy and fear. I also remember thinking that this kind of thing happened to sweaty men in too-tight safari pants in documentaries about the Serengeti. Not in Hove. To a normal person who actively avoids tight safari shorts.

Was there a button I could press to turn this off? Unfortunately not. So I started running. All the while my friend was wetting himself laughing at what, for me, was quickly degenerating into a code-red situation. It took a while, but it slowly dawned on me that if I turned left or right then that might vex the heifer. As it turned out, this was the solution. Unfortunately, it took just a bit too long to figure that out because for a good thirty metres I was engaged in a foot pursuit that efficiently stripped me of the notions of reason and personal dignity to which I had previously clung. Once again, as with other segments in this book, I am not particularly proud of my reaction. I had been pursued by a cow and, due to my inability to consider turning left or right, I had also been out-thought by a cow. A cow had set me a mental challenge and I had failed to come up with the goods. Don't let it happen to you. Turn left or right.

Don't be a nudist

'But it's the most natural thing in the world to walk around naked.' Except it's not really, is it?

Don't avoid the doctor if you have a lump

Finding a lump on one of your balls is not a nice thing. On the list of things that are nice to appear on your balls (itself a pretty small and select list) it comes at the bottom next to a piranha and an industrial vice. I have had this dubious pleasure twice and have twice been faced with the prospect of approaching the medical fraternity. In such circumstances the best-case scenario is that you get your balls very purposefully played with by a man who feels even more uncomfortable about it than you do and then confirms that it is a cyst. Now, having seen a few different practitioners, I feel I am something of an authority on the subject of what makes a good and bad GP when it comes to seeing someone about a lump downstairs. I have made a list for anyone who finds themselves in this scenario in the future.

When you first find a lump you will probably spend a week or two telling yourself that it has been there forever, that it is a tiny cyst. You'll do some internet research where you type search strings like, 'Lump on my balls' into Google in the hope that Google will respond with, 'Don't worry, Carl, it's definitely a benign cyst. No need for someone to play with your balls after all.' But of course Google won't do that and you know, even at this point, that you are on a fast track to having a man play with your testicles in a medical setting.

There might be an intervening GP appointment where you try to get your doctor to say the words, 'Most lumps are harmless and yours certainly is,' without actually mentioning your testicles or the lump there. And that is not easy, let me tell you. However, so lame is this that you might as well go in and tell him that a 'friend' has a lump. For example, I went in to tell my GP that I had a sore stomach (which I did). He noted that I had a new bike and that it could have led to a stomach strain. I was deeply satisfied with this explanation and left the surgery without considering that new bikes tend not to grow lumps on your nuts in the space of a week. Upon this basic realization I was back in there a week later.

Now I happen to have experience of two doctors reacting to the words, 'I think I have a lump,' and, while their finger dexterity could not have been more different, I saw in both the same look of strangled horror that most male doctors probably feel when they hear those words. The plastic gloves come on and you both find yourselves talking about cricket, the weather, the weather and cricket – everything really, apart from the fact that you have a professional medic on his knees, kneading your testicles.

One of my doctors responded with fingers supple and gentle enough for me to almost be mistaken that it was me touching my balls. Quite an achievement. The other manhandled me like my balls had grown a larynx and called his wife a slut. I yelled on three separate occasions, wondering if he was actually conducting the operation to remove the lump there and then. If there is something there you will often get a further referral. Then you know that that was just the beginning of your monumental discomfort.

The referral

Once it has happened more than once you feel like a veteran, like you should be saying 'Hi' to the receptionists and asking after their families. You begin to take on the identity of the old sea dog of the ultrasound ward. Whereas first time round you feel like you are wearing a sign that says, 'I don't think my balls work, can someone help me?', the second time you feel like reassuring the nearest ultrasound virgin with your prior knowledge. Most importantly, the second time you don't think it's going to be cancer, whereas the first time you are thinking about who is going to get your guitar.

Both times I have been met by an overly enthusiastic ultrasound technician whose desperation to make me feel at home, with the best intentions in the world, actually made me feel like I was the first man going in for an operation to have a breast sewn onto his forehead. He was frantically normalizing the scenario, whilst at the same time clearly betraying his own nervous apprehension. This approach made me feel like I had better not disappoint him, that I should see it as one of the most comfortable but routine experiences of my life. Like a holiday to Butlins, except one where a stranger stares at your groin and then puts cold gel on it.

The second appointment had a junior female nurse in tow. Of course, I was asked if I would mind her being in the room, told that she was training and advised that it would be 'particularly useful' for her. It is possibly a reflection of my state of mind at the time, but the use of the phrase 'particularly useful' gave me the unnerving feeling that my balls would offer her a greater training ground than the other sets of balls that were popping through the door that day or week. I couldn't think why. They weren't particularly big and even I could tell that the lump wasn't a whopper that you might sit on a golf tee in a careless moment. So I calmed down, reasoning that it was just a poor turn of phrase feeding my paranoia. Anyway, the trainee nurse was more embarrassed than me and her eyes had to be guided between my balls and the ultrasound screen like a naughty child being made to look at the damage she has caused by an angry mother. So we had a trainee desperate not to look at what she was supposed to be learning, a patient being politely browbeaten into seeming not only calm and relaxed but like he was enjoying the process, and a ringmaster overseeing both. A curious interaction indeed.

I also noticed a marked difference between the amount of gel placed on my balls on the two separate occasions. I remember this because it's not every day that I look down to see my balls doing backstroke in a river of ultrasound gel. I'm not sure if this was down to the advancement in technology (there was a ten-year difference between visits), but the second man just laid them on a paper towel and went to work, whereas the first looked like he'd been asked to juggle a number of Vaseline-coated fish. He could not get hold of them for love nor money. I thought about offering to help, but my embarrassment had changed to confusion and then finally curiosity as I wondered how, and indeed if, he would actually regain control of these gel-soaked plums. It was like dunking for apples and I was taken back to the Halloween parties of my childhood. This was a useful mental diversion as the technician fought to regain control of his professional dignity. I thought he might have to bring out a fishing net, but eventually he was back in the saddle and we were off.

Things that good and bad GPs will do when you consult them about a lump on your balls

- A good GP will reassure you that, even though you need an ultrasound, it is probably a false alarm.
- A bad GP will say, 'Is this it?' a number of times as you beg, through screaming fits, for an epidural.
- A good GP will politely ask you to lift your penis out of the way so that he can carry out his check.
- A bad GP will hold on to your penis throughout the examination like someone has asked him to grab hold of a lump of leprosy.
- A good GP will use reassuring words, pat you on the back for being brave enough to come and tell you that not enough men seek help.
- A bad GP will say, 'OK, let's have a little play downstairs then.'
- A good GP will talk you through the procedure and explain what he is assessing.
- A bad GP will say in a saucy voice, 'I should be charging for this!' when he is handling you.
- A good GP will tell you the statistics for false alarms and successful treatments.
- A bad GP will say, 'Tell you what, I'll get mine out too so we all feel comfortable.'

Don't tell other men how to put an animal out of its misery

I happen to know a number of officers of the law. By some curious twist of fate a disproportionate number of people I know have decided to take it upon themselves to protect and to serve. One of said number recently told me about an ugly incident that occurred on a shift. They had been called out at 4 a.m. to a country road where a man had swerved into a tree whilst trying to avoid hitting a deer. The man was in quite a bad way, although not critical, but the deer was less fortunate. It had clearly been hurt beyond repair and in the end a vet had been called out to put the poor creature down. The reason I mention this run-of-the-mill incident is that my police contact was later told by a fellow (male) officer that he should just have put the deer out of its misery by himself, that there had been no need to trouble a vet for his services. Quite reasonably, my friend enquired as to exactly how he was supposed to have achieved this. He was informed that he should have strangled it.

That's right, he should have strangled it. Now just think about that for a second. My police friend is more patient and less sarcastic than I because my immediate thought would have been, 'Ah, good idea, but I wasn't sure which of my eleven deer-strangling techniques, that I've received extensive training on, would be the most appropriate in this instance.' What would have happened had he followed this cucumber's advice? He would have been sat at the side of the road for aeons trying, unsuccessfully, to strangle an already ailing deer while a badly hurt man trapped in a car wondered why he had been saved by a very stupid man cuddling a critically ill deer. Could there possibly be a less effective and less dignified way of spending police time?

There is a breed of man out there who has absolute confidence in matters of makeshift animal husbandry despite their pet fish constituting their entire history of experience with animals. Odd.

Don't think for a second that you can handle yourself

Most men suffer from one enormous fallacy about themselves. It starts from a young age and continues all the way through their lives unless they are unlucky enough to happen upon circumstances that contradict this particular part of their personal identity. Or they get a bit older and grow up a bit, at which point they naturally start to realize that they have been labouring under a grave misconception. If you asked most guys how hard they were or how they'd fare in a fight, the majority would probably mumble something about being able to handle themselves. Ask them to rate themselves on a scale of one to ten and most would probably say somewhere around a six. And of course they would be wrong. Because hardness doesn't work on a linear interval scale like this. The scale only has two groups: one to three and eight to ten. There is no middle. You are either hard or you are soft. It doesn't matter whether you work out, whether you do martial arts, or whether you are exceptionally tall. What matters is anger, simple as that. If you are capable of summoning ferocious anger in a split second, you are hard. If not, you're soft. End of story.

Don't take a gap year to 'go travelling'

Have a think about the following questions:

- Do you have a secret or even quite public yearning to 'find yourself'?
- Are you able to be exposed to visions of galling poverty, come back, forget all about it and work in wealthy western institutions?
- Do you think you will be able to explain away such galling poverty as part and parcel of the rustic charm of the smiley native people?
- Does your family have quite a lot, a lot or an awful lot of money?
- Would you like to smoke cannabis without 'suits' getting in the way and telling you not to?
- Do you believe that getting drunk, stoned and spending two weeks at a time with Australian strangers in tourist Meccas in the Far East will enable you to learn about the world?
- Are you prepared to spend the six months following your trip wearing a mix of ethnic and western clothes that allow you to express your new wisdom?
- And then stop it when you get bored?
- Are you concerned that you don't use the word 'like' anywhere near enough (as in, 'Like, whatever, man')?
- Would you like to make everything you say sound like a question?

If the answer to any, some or all of these questions is yes then you are ready to go travelling. Otherwise you could do something worthwhile.

Don't go to 'amusement' arcades

When I was a child I used to marvel at the amusement arcade on Kilmarnock high street and on the seafronts of our traditional holiday destinations. For me, holidays to Morecambe yielded many benchmark experiences, from my first ever real time alone (walking along the seafront listening to the Pet Shop Boys' 'Suburbia') to being forced to apologize to a fuming couple after enquiring from our B&B window (at my older brother's *command*), whether they were, or were not, c***s. But the one element that always stood out so clearly was the excitement of the big amusement arcades. The only thing I can remember being more exciting than a massive (and I mean gargantuan) cut-out of Jim Bowen's head in Morecambe was their glorious and yet forbidden allure. Those dark little caverns filled with men playing one-armed bandits and children watching a metal hand fail miserably to cling on to what looked like a cheap toy guinea pig. The windows, draped in glitter and tinsel, provided an enticing glimpse of some of the treasures within, like cheap watches, plastic-looking jewellery and frying pan sets. I dreamt of the time when I too could go in there and lose a series of two pence pieces on a moving ridge.

As I got a little older, however, the allure of the tinsel, Jim Bowen and the metal hand that couldn't scratch its own metal dick (had it one) gradually wore off. I started to realize that, other than bored teenagers, the only people who seemed to go to these arcades of amusement were middle-aged men in tracksuit trousers who were wearing tracksuit trousers on account of the fact that they had been going into amusement arcades for too long. The wonder and glee that had filled my young mind was replaced with pity and sorrow at the lives wasted away in front of flashing machines that will always beat you in the end. The sight of desperate, grown men using two-penny fruit machines is simply heartbreaking.

Don't play the bongos

As with so many things in life, if I am confused about something I ask myself, 'What would Sting do?' and then choose the alternative. Now I have never met Sting. I'm sure he is a perfectly nice man; this just happens to work as a rule of thumb for me on the big decisions in my life. So, do the bongo drums pass my Sting test? No chance, he loves them.

Don't do martial arts

I remember when I was nine years old my friend Gary and I used to watch a series called *The Master*. The show focused on the adventures of an aging ninja master, played by Lee Van Cleef, and his young pupil. Much like the *A-Team*, the mismatched pair would drive around in a customized van, helping people in need (and their always-stunning niece/daughter) along the way. Which was great. Gary and I used to play the two characters and, after dark, we would jump from car to car pretending to be ninjas. I should note at this juncture that this was Kilmarnock in Scotland in the 1980s and there was not a great market for nine-year-old ninjas. We didn't take this personally. Anyway, one of us would pretend to be a nefarious passer-by and the other would jump off a car and attack him with a stick. At this point, a very poorly choreographed martial arts fight between a nine-year-old pretend ninja and an eight-year-old pretend 'hood' would unfold. We found this both entertaining and gratifying. We would pretend to be armed with throwing stars (stones), kendo sticks (normal sticks) and nunchucks (normal sticks tied with a shoelace) and use these uniquely odd and inefficient weapons to attack each other while trying to sound Japanese.

Now what do you think the key phrase in the above tale is? Is it that, 'We pretended to be ninjas'? Or that, 'We had pretend weapons'? Nope. The key phrase in that excerpt is, 'When I was nine years old'. For many children martial arts is a big thing. Martial arts, and the accompanying ninja lore, allows incumbents to imagine themselves as stealthy, fast and tough, able to perform feats of climbing and jumping that most house cats would struggle with. Perfect for a nine-year-old.

If you ask children interested in engaging in martial arts why they do it and/or why they watch martial arts films you'll probably receive some pretty honest answers about how they want to be ninjas, want to be able to deliver a round-house kick to the face of the kid who stole their lunch or how they want to be known by classmates as being really hard. Amazingly, these motivations don't change for adult male martial artists (although by now people are unlikely to be stealing their lunch). These paragons of arrested development feel exactly the same way, but of course they can't say that they secretly want to be ninjas or want to be thought of as really hard, because people will assume that they are unwell. So if you ask adult men why they do martial arts you will hear various vague mumblings about discipline and fitness and self-control. They will tell you that martial arts provide good discipline and that they help you to stay in tip-top shape. What I want to know is a) why they need to be disciplined in the first place and b) how exactly regularly kicking an estate agent and a plumber in the balls in a municipal town hall on a Monday provides this discipline?

The main problem with martial arts is that they attract the kind of men who, no matter how many times they are taught about discipline and restraint, cannot defeat the urge to show other men that they are, in fact, hard. Modern social norms dictate that these guys are unable to display their teak-tough physical prowess and so they choose increasingly elaborate and unusual ways to do it. My favourite is the one where one of them holds some wood and another hits it really hard until it breaks. In the whole history of man I can think of few less impressive displays of physical power than watching one silly man hit a bit of wood that he has convinced another silly man to hold. And I always have the same thought: that I could also achieve this feat, but that it would really hurt, just like it really hurts them. Of course, they would respond that the difference between my feminized, limp flesh and their wolverine-like wrists means that it doesn't actually hurt them. But, you see, it does. I know it does, they know it does and deep down I think that they know that I know. So being able to break a piece of wood is not the skill here. The skill seems to be the ability to do something silly that hurts you without shouting out in pain. And that surely has to be one of the most redundant skills a human can have. Right up there with the ability to masturbate using only the soles of your feet and juggling (the former of which I hold in greater esteem than the latter).

Anyway, since when have you been jumped at a bus stop late at night by a group of savage hooligans chasing you with blocks of wood held conveniently above their heads that they are desperate for someone to smash and pretend that it doesn't hurt? I'm not saying that it never happens, just that I don't remember ever having seen it. If this happened, then I really could under-stand the need for this 'skill'. However, if I remember rightly, these hooligans tend to have knives, baseball bats and other such accoutrements that they will attempt to cleave to your skull. Perhaps you've been in a heaving pub when some seven foot monster rounds on you for staring at his girlfriend's

breasts. 'Right, you little fucker, were you staring at my bird's tits? Cos if you were I'm gonna take you outside and make you hit a piece of two by four and pretend it doesn't hurt.'

Don't leap over gates that you can clearly walk through

Let's picture a scene. You are having a nice country walk with a friend or some friends, perhaps enjoying the bracing air of the Sussex Downs, the rugged landscape of Dartmoor, or the beautiful vistas of the Pennines. You are walking along, talking away, when you approach a fence with a gate. And then it happens. You don't want it to, you gave no intimation that you wanted it to happen, but it does anyway. One of your colleagues vaults over the fence when he could clearly just have gone through the gate.

Now I have been party to this experience on a number of occasions and each time I was immediately hit by a plethora of thoughts and emotions. Like a nasty racist slur or a sickeningly misogynistic detail of a sexual encounter, it is one of those galling instances when your acquaintance does or says something that makes you belatedly realize that you are in the company of an idiot.

So why do they do it? Why would a man repeatedly jump over a fence or gate that he could quite simply walk through? When this happens, beware the pretence that it wasn't done for effect. The protagonist will look around casually as if something important has suddenly caught their eye in the distance and their recent act of physical heroics will be framed by an insouciant attitude of, 'Like, yeah, whatever man, get over it. I nailed the jump, move on.' But even though it doesn't bother him, you will be racked with pain over the knowledge that there was gate. That's right, there was a gate. There was a gate that he could have walked through. And don't say it is easier to jump. It never, ever is. Even if the gate is a moving target being pulled around by a plucky trickster with a jester's hat, it's still easier than the vault.

When thought through logically, it is actually one of the most profound insults that someone could throw at you. This is because in their brain they have done a few calculations. They have weighed up the pros and cons, thought about past circumstances, present company, the current circumstances, and your intellectual capacity and they have concluded that this course of action will impress you. That's right; they have decided that you will be impressed by an adult male who can jump over a fence. That you are so simple that this course of action will make you think that this person is somehow 'good'. I would actually be less insulted if, when we approached the fence, he just turned round, rolled up his sleeve and furiously flexed his bicep right in front of me, and then moved on without comment or explanation. At least then we could dispense with the insultingly nonchalant post-vault countenance. And this starts a train of thought: what other things does he think I might be impressed by? Arm-wrestling children with rickets? Fighting someone smaller than you when they're not looking? Throwing a ball a long way? Counting to ten really quickly? Swearing at a passer-by and then pointing to someone else? Don't do it, folks.

Don't design security fences

'Hey, Tom, how's things, buddy?'

'Yeah good, Richard, yourself?'

'Oh, you know, same old, same old.'

'Wife and kids?'

'Never been better, thanks, Tom. Listen, mate, I'm interested in getting a new security fence for the yard, but I'm not really sure where to start, if you know what I mean.'

'Oh, no problem, Richard, and why should you? After all, that's my job.'

'Only there are some kids who have been hanging around the warehouse recently and I'm keen that we don't lose any material. You know we had that break-in last year. God forbid that happens again.'

'I understand completely, mate, say no more. I just need to go through a series of questions. You know, standard procedure and all that. Now, would you like it to tear into their balls or just around them?'

'Er... I don't know. Torn into, I suppose.'

'Once torn into their balls, do you want the spike to rotate so that their scrotums are stretched insufferably?'

'Erm... I guess not, I don't know, I mean, they are only kids.'

'Think about the yard, Richard, think about the yard; let's keep our eyes on the prize here. OK, would you like their arse, balls or arse *and* balls to be impaled? We actually have one that will pull them apart; literally, I mean it will be like Hiroshima down there. You wouldn't even know he was a boy. And what about the fishhook design which basically means that they can't unhook without the fire brigade and incredibly well-qualified and patient surgeons? They are going like hotcakes at the moment, and aesthetically they are little stunners. The page-three gals of the anti-scale barrier world.'

'I suppose I'll have one of those then.'

'Now, do you want them to retain the option of breeding when they are older?'

'Well, yeah, I mean, I just want them off the yard.'

'Hmmm. I wasn't going to mention this, but we have a new model with a revolving Taser-charged cat-o'-nine-tails. Whips them while they get electrocuted to the point of incontinence. It can be messy but it sends out the right signals.'

'But can people see this just by looking?'

'Oh no, God no, they have no idea, none at all. The first they'll know is when they are skewered like a Burberry kebab. I mean, are you really serious about these vandals? We can even chuck in some barbed wire around the edges, just as a bit of trim to set it off.'

'Do you do CCTV too?'

'Oh God, yeah, you're going to want to watch it at the Christmas party.'

'Well, erm, I suppose that's all. Just invoice me and we'll sort it out.'

'Bye, Richard.'

'OK, bye, Tom.'

Now we don't currently live in a post-apocalyptic wasteland where crazed heathens roam a desolate, charred landscape, sacrificing all and sundry, à la *Mad Max II*. If Lord Humungus, warrior of the wasteland, was to design these – a man whose daily routine involved scalping minions and walking a half-human around on a chain like a dog – then I could get it, it would make perfect sense. But he does not. They are designed by a normal man in a normal suit who goes to work in a normal car. Perhaps he has a side-parting and flecks of grey; on his desk sits a stapler, an apple and a photo of Mary and the kids when they were camping last year in Devon. Perhaps he likes to do *The Times* crossword and plays a round of golf or two in his spare time when the weather allows. What separates him from other mild-mannered office workers all over the country? What separates him is that he spends every working hour thinking about, designing and visualizing different ways to tear a man's scrotum to shreds. Then, at the end of the day, he puts on his duffle coat, hops in his Ford Sierra and drives home for dinner. Am I the only one a little disconcerted by this picture?

'OK, Mr Wilson, why don't you go ahead and tell the class what you do?'
'Well, children, I am a fireman, I help people in trouble and put out fires before they can hurt people.'
(Children cheer and clap.)
'And what about you, Mr Baron?'
'Well, kids, I am an estate agent. When your mum and dad want to buy a new house I help them to get the nicest house they can.'
(Children smile and clap although the smart ones will eye him with suspicion.)
'And what about you, Mr Green?'
'Well, kids, I spend day after day after day thinking of new ways to make sure that teenage vandals have their balls, dicks, arseholes and both legs torn like ten-day-old kebabs on rotating anti-scale barriers with inverted three-pronged fishhook spikes.'

It's not right.

Don't hand out advice on how to protect yourself against animals

I recently came across an article which outlined the action you should take to protect yourself from angry cows if you are caught out on a walk in the country. Apparently you don't look them in the eye, you stay on the path, keep twenty metres away, and keep dogs on a leash. Moreover, as a last resort, if you do get attacked, you should aim a well-placed strike to the cow's nose. Now I love advice like this. Strike it on the nose. I can't help thinking I've already lost this particular battle if my only option left is to strike the thing on its face. Call me old-fashioned but I am a little uneasy at engaging a cow in a fist fight. What if it is blocking your way? Do you just walk up to it and punch it in the face? Could work, I suppose, but again I'm not sure that I feel that comfortable doing this. I did a bit of Tae Kwon Do once. Does kicking count too? Can I kick it in the face? Or is this just absurd?

'Hi love, how was your walk?'
'Oh it was great, air was beautiful, the heather was out, the sun was shining. Absolutely delightful. Oh and I round-house kicked a cow right in the mush.'
'Did you drop any cows with a left hook?'
'No, just the round-house kick today love, right on the gob.'

Doesn't fit, does it? Like many other people, I consider myself a reasonably intelligent person with at least a modicum of civic class. I find the idea of punching a cow in the face a little bit degrading. Like tripping up a baby or letting down the tyres of one of those buggies that old people use to knock pedestrians over. They also say that you should be careful if their young are around. Great, thanks for that. Do I take a member of bovine social services with me to prove my good intentions?

Don't dress like Indiana Jones

What do you think when you see a man walking down the street wearing a trilby hat? Or perhaps a man wearing a long, black, leather trench coat? When I see someone wearing a trilby I feel that we have an automatic connection. I think that we implicitly agree on one thing: that Indiana Jones makes a trilby look cool. He really does. Together with the whip and the leather jacket it screams 'heroic man of adventure'. When I see Keanu Reeves wearing a long, black, leather coat in *The Matrix* I think that his look is indeed fitting of 'Neo', the chosen one. However, I do not have these thoughts when I see an estate agent from Bournemouth or a teacher from Derby donning these garments.

And yet there is a special breed of man who believes that he can carry off what can only really be described as movie clothing. These are men for whom the line between reality and film is a little more blurred than for the rest of us. Where we see these films as ninety minutes of entertainment that allow us to willingly suspend our disbelief, the trilby wearer sees them as prescriptions for everyday style. At some stage he has the thought, 'If Indy can do it, why can't I?' However, he ignores two things. Firstly, he ignores the fact that he doesn't look like Harrison Ford. More importantly, he ignores the fact that certain clothes need a certain lifestyle to justify them. The looks in question can only fit if the wearer is engaged in a world of reckless adventure, peril and cavalier heroism. Using these clothes to get from the train station to your work at the council office on a wet Tuesday morning really doesn't work.

Don't talk in a hairdresser's unless you're a professional small-talker

A hairdresser's is not just a hairdresser's. If all that happened inside a hairdresser's was that you had your haircut then I would be a very happy bunny. But it's not. It is manifestly not what it says on the proverbial tin. It is a haircut PLUS a period of very public, often excruciating and usually unavoidable small-talk. And it's small-talk that will be scrutinized by a group of bored punters because your small-talk is the only thing that stands between them and a re-reading of the latest society wedding stories from *OK* magazine. And, good God, it can be a minefield.

My problem is that I'm not very good at it. This is particularly problematic when your turn comes after someone who is clearly a semi-professional small-talker, turning out funny little tidbits in response to the most mundane questions. You watch in awe as he belts out hairdresser shop humour with all the fluidity of a redcoat. Then it's your turn. Of course, you try to bring your A-game but, since you're following the town's answer to Stephen Fry, the hairdresser understandably loses interest. Sometimes I half-expect the hairdresser to call to a more junior colleague, 'Hi, Gene, could you take over here? this one's boring.' No, it's better to follow someone who is manifestly dull or has poor personal hygiene. At least then you are a step in the right direction, even if your small-talk could anesthetize an ADHD child on speed. The moral of the story is either to be good at it or if you can't be good at it then shut your mouth and stare at the floor. Better to be thought of as rude than boring.

Don't tell other men how bright your children are. Ever.

So there you are at a party; it could be any sort of social gathering. You're chatting away to a number of people you don't know very well. There are kids running around and so, naturally, the conversation of children comes up. Maybe the odd word about local schools, good teachers, bad teachers and so on. Then perhaps people begin to mention their own children, some of their experiences, the good points of being a parent and some funny stories about their kids. So far, so good.

Then it happens. Almost from nowhere, one member of your circle (and this can be a stranger, a family member, a friend, a work colleague – literally anyone) starts to do it. You feel a nauseating malaise gently build, your stomach drops and your arse begins to slowly hurt. First with a kind of numb feeling, the physical manifestation of boredom and nausea combined. It then moves to a full-on, raw ache as you realize your rank powerlessness in the hellish scenario that is unfolding. You start to perspire gently. This quickly moves to a full-on sweat. You look around, desperation in your eyes. A desperation that begs someone, anyone, to save you. Right now you would rather listen to people's holiday stories ('This was Paco, he was our barman. He was soooo funny. One night he …' etc. etc.) than be engulfed in this very private social death. But it's too late. You are now officially listening to a father boast about his child.

Is this boasting based on his child being able to solve the riddle of the space-time continuum and finally elucidate the complex philosophical and mathematical implications of the Big Bang? Or perhaps he has found the way to understand the physiological and emotional secret of human consciousness? No, it turns out he has put a block in a hole of a cheap plastic toy.

These men are committing two crimes against conversational etiquette in one. Firstly, by boasting, which in itself is not very nice to have to listen to, and secondly, by talking incessantly about a subject on which the listener probably has very little real interest - someone else's child. Hell, why not go all the way and tell the listener how good you are in bed too. That you can sustain an unusually firm erection for a length of time that would make Charlie Sheen double-take.

Even if the child *is* bright, why would I actually care? And why do so few boasting fathers ask themselves this question? At some point did I say that I had a couple of really testing child puzzles that I could use some help with if anyone's child was up to the task? No, I don't think so. Perhaps I made a general plea for someone to bore me until my balls ached? No, I don't recall that one either. I know, I must have asked if there was anyone in the group who could prove they had really good genes. Hmmm, actually, now that I think of it, I didn't mention that either. In that case, it must mean that I DON'T CARE HOW SMART YOUR CHILD IS.

Don't let a Womble share your moment of glory at the end of a marathon

Back in my slightly sprightlier youth I took it upon myself to run the London Marathon. I used to jog quite a bit and at the time I lived in London so it made sense that I would one day end up having a crack at the marathon. So I trained for a number of months, bought some nice trainers and various items of thermal and Lycra clothing and set forth to conquer the twenty-six-and-a-bit miles around our capital. Well, I won't lie to you, reader, if you have had the pleasure of never undertaking such a pursuit, it was hard. Really, really hard. By twenty miles I was running like Bambi after a road-traffic accident. It was ugly. My legs felt like wood and every step was a new and sustained form of agony that felt like my legs were trying to give birth to newer, younger legs that might be slightly less shit.

Anyway, towards the end I wasn't a picture of health mentally – more or less reduced to crying for my mum for the last three miles. My previous enthusiasm for bringing respite to the elderly of the country as a runner for the Age Concern charity gave way to my casually swearing under my breath every time I saw an old person. My fatigued mind had managed to convince itself that they were the problem; it was they who made me endure this perpetual agony just so they could get their grubby little mitts on a few hundred pounds for shiny new Zimmer frames. Big-eared bastards. However, one thought and one thought only sustained me. That thought was of the finish line, of getting my hands on that little medal and having my celebratory photo of my shambling frame victoriously crossing the line. I was the first person I knew to do the marathon and I knew that the final photograph of my crossing the line would be a little souvenir that I could keep forever. As such, I got to the line and raised my arms in the air, exhausted but proud.

Three weeks later the photograph arrived through the post and I eagerly opened it, ready for a pictorial representation of my masculine power. And sure enough it showed me, fatigued, sweating, in visible pain and crossing the line with my arms in the air. I looked dreadful, but I had made it. However, a closer inspection of the photo highlighted a problem. Do you know who was next to me? A really, really old woman, who had clearly crossed the line just in front of me and looked like she had been out for a morning stroll. And she was *old*. This woman would have been mistaken for Barbara Cartland's mother had the two been standing together at a bus stop. But the problem was that she looked much, much better than me. Needless to say, the photograph was immediately useless. You get no social plaudits for displaying a photo which shows that a frighteningly old woman, whose previous greatest achievement had been avoiding death, has more physical resilience than you. With slightly dented pride and no shortage of disap-pointment I resolved to one day do the marathon again.

Sure enough, a few years later I did just that with a good friend who was running it for the first time. The one piece of advice I gave him? Forget the training, the eating and the equipment. I told him that the most important thing was to make sure he had a good look around before he came through the line. I didn't want him to become a victim of a freak geriatric phenom-enon like I was. My friend bore this in mind and in his last 200 yards he looked around him, just to make sure. And what did he see? He saw a Womble. Well, not literally a Womble, but a man in a Womble costume. However, we will refer to him as the Womble. Realizing that he didn't want his achievement similarly tarnished, he resolved not to share photo-space with said Womble. And so he sped up. He gave everything he had so that he could have a photo that he and his family were proud of, the photo that I was so cruelly and brutally denied. In an ideal world this would be the end of this story, but it's not. Why not? Because the Womble saw what was happening and responded. My friend found himself at the end of the biggest running race on earth in search of a fitting memorial for his physical prowess but to do this he had been reduced to racing a Womble. As it happens, I think that the Womble dipped on the line but, ironically, you needed a photo finish to separate them. Just like me, his moment of glory had been tarnished.

Don't play fruit machines

Can there really be any greater signifier of the moribund emptiness of modern living in the twenty-first century than the pub fruit machine? On a boat trip to Belgium with a group of friends some years ago I experienced the same epiphany that Sarah Connor experiences in the *Terminator* films. That dawning realization that the human race is, in fact, utterly doomed to extinction. Moreover, there is absolutely nothing we can do about it. Whereas Sarah Connor had a mental breakdown and decided to grow twenty-one inch biceps through doing chin-ups in the local asylum in preparation for the apocalypse, I just tutted and had another lager.

The sight that made me realize the futility of our future was not the presence of killer robots who would enslave and murder the human race, but that of two friends playing a French fruit machine (of sorts) on the ship over. I sat watching them plough euro after euro into a slot machine that looked like a cross between a fruit machine and a pinball machine without flippers. They put money in and a ball was released, it moved down from the top of the tilted board to the bottom, but the 'player' had no obvious way to interfere with the ball's progress (à la pinball) and hence generate amusement. Basically, they had no control whatsoever of the ball. My friends could not figure out how the game worked, how to influence the ball or how to win money, but they continued to throw euros into this contraption, regardless, like they were the currency of the devil. Sure enough, they would put the cash in the slot, watch a ball being released, follow it down to the bottom of the board and then look at each other. A small time gap (that clearly wasn't used for reflection) would be followed by one or other of them putting some more money in the machine. All the time they were talking about how they were going to hit it big, that the payout was just round the corner and that they were on the edge of figuring this thing out. I watched their dedicated persistence in ignoring the fact that there was no slot to collect money from should they suddenly succeed in telepathically altering the course of the ball. When they finally had no money left they just sat and stared at the machine, as if it would start throwing the ball down of its own accord in gratitude at their financial investment in its curious formulation of entertainment. And as they sat and stared, transfixed by the flashing lights and the now-stationary ball, I realized that one day, soon, we are all going to die. The human race simply cannot sustain this kind of behaviour and survive.

Do not wear comedy ties

Like Uri Geller's career longevity in bizarre entertainment anticlimaxes, the continued survival of comedy ties as a sartorial option is one of the great mysteries of the modern age. The time to mince words is over. The wearers of comedy ties are amongst the most dangerous creatures to roam offices the planet over. I would sooner share a cage with an arctic tiger than a man who wears comedy ties. Yup, that's right, a snow tiger, and with big teeth, too. Like the one that ate Siegfried or Roy.

The problem is that comedy-tie man has absolutely no concept of fun, how it works and where it operates. This man compartmentalizes fun and lightheartedness like he would compartmentalize a visit to the gym or the dentist. He believes not only that he can represent fun in the form of a comedy tie but that fun can now be ticked off of his list of things to do for the day. 'OK, today I put on my comedy tie and so I had fun. Next?' Of course, fun doesn't work like this in practice. It tends to happen *to* us and if you want to make it happen it needs a little more work than a cartoon picture of a pint of beer on a tie. This is especially the case at work. The comedy tie betrays a fundamental misunderstanding of what fun actually is and it ends up acting as a red alert that, in your midst, is a man who wouldn't know humour if it break-danced up to him dressed head to feet in comedy ties.

Don't worry about not knowing as much as other men

I would imagine that, unless you are the pipe-smoking, bearded encyclopaedia who constantly beats me in any pub quiz I enter, you have been in a social situation where you are chatting to some friends or work colleagues and suddenly someone casually drops a name that you should probably know but don't. Maybe it's Sartre, or Goddard, or Marx, maybe it's Glenn Hoddle. Hell, it could be anyone. You know you should have a working knowledge of this person, but you don't. The normal thing to do is to sit tight, hope that the conversation moves on sharpish and that your intellectual ignorance survives another day free of revelation. This tactic has served me well on the countless occasions that my ignorance has made me a conversational passenger. But sometimes this isn't enough. Sometimes you get a sinking feeling in the pit of your stomach as you realize that being a passenger just isn't going to cut it on this occasion. An alarm bell has gone off and you are going to have to respond.

OK, so the conversation has drifted out of your league and you are now slap bang in the middle of a social emergency. Step one, don't panic. Nod your head slowly but firmly in a non-committed fashion to whoever is talking. Occasionally squint your eyes and look perplexed. Give them the feeling that, although not altogether in agreement with them, you are willing to let them continue to expand on their point. This looks like you are on top of it.

Still talking? Move to step two. Surreptitiously train your eyes on the brightest person in the group. If they are nodding in agreement then do so too, but with even more vigour. Likewise, if they are shaking their head. You may even want to say, 'Not sure I agree with that,' and hope that you're not challenged but that the brighter person who also disagrees with the speaker takes up the fight on your behalf. If they do, look like you were about to speak but held back in the name of social courtesy and are willing to let the brighter person make the case.

If this comment is challenged, move to step three. Now you have to conjure the ancient art of saying something that doesn't mean anything. For instance, you might try, 'It just seems that you are being narrow in your analysis,' and hope that they then expand in greater depth. If you get away with this, do not disagree again. This is a close shave. However, if this doesn't work it's on to step four.

Step four should only be used in absolute emergencies. Shout, 'I'm not even going to have this conversation and you know why', and storm out of the room. You might be followed, so prepare to think quickly about why their point was somehow construed as a challenge to a dead relative when the wounds are still too tender to go there. Say you thought they knew this and were being insensitive. For instance, 'You know my grandad was a Marx scholar, you had no right to bring this up.' Then apologize for being over-sensitive. Nobody will bring the name up again.

Don't tell people that time management is a skill

But, hang on, I hear you say. Some guys just can't help it, it's just their way. Some find it very difficult to manage their time and so should receive sympathy and help.

No, no and no again. For the hard of thinking, and despite what human resource mandarins who have managed to elevate time-management courses to the zenith of job creation exercises tell us, YOU CANNOT MANAGE TIME. It just is. Time just is. There is no such thing as a time-management problem. What people manage is what they do during a certain period of time and what these guys have to learn to work on is their 'don't give a fuck' management. Ice skating is a skill, archery is a skill; there are things that people have to be taught. Time management is not a skill. You just take a look at your watch and try not to be a prick. Voila! People who really don't want to be late for a meeting or appointment or event with another person have the benefit of various technological devices. For instance, they can set an alarm. Simple. If you are not very good at being aware of what is happening in your life, simply set an alarm. There is no element of skill here, no inherent ability. Just a simple case of whether you can be bothered to treat someone with a bit of consideration.

Flashers don't have clothes-management issues. Their clothes don't just fall off because they didn't do them up right. Bank robbers don't have 'correct way to behave in a bank' management issues. They don't reach to pull out their cheque book and grab a pair of tights and an AK47 by mistake. Equating men who are perpetually late with flashers and bank robbers may seem extreme, but they have one key thing in common. Punctuality has a very simple explanation – despite the punctuality-apologist industry that has obfuscated this simple truth – poor punctuality is intentional. These men were late to meet someone once and had a choice there and then as to whether it became a habit. By choosing not to put anything in place to prevent this in future they have decided that it will happen again and that this is OK. Time management is not a skill.

Do not ride fold-up bikes

First thing's first. Cycling shorts were designed for cycling. This may seem obvious, but it needs to be stated here. In every other environment they are the most bizarre and obscene item of clothing in the western world. But luckily there is an unwritten rule about cycling shorts that we all adhere to, a kind of social contract. Just as we all offer our hand if someone offers theirs and don't talk to strange men at urinals, we have an implicit rule for cycling shorts. This rule is that you wear them on bikes. Simple. Except, of course, for our fold-up bike user. Oh no. He smashes this rule with impunity. He gets onto a busy train, packs his stupid, stupid bike into a matchbox – or whatever they use – tumbles through the central aisle of the train and sits down. That he is the walking equivalent of a man wearing a full astronaut's outfit just to *look* at the moon seems not to worry him. Now if that was where the problem ended I could probably live with these guys.

But I can see his balls. That's right, more often than not I can count the pubic hairs on his balls through the Lycra. Now smite me for being old-fashioned, but in my cloistered world it is fundamentally inconsiderate to a) show your balls in public or b) stand next to someone with your groin at the level of their head so that they have a big pair of barely concealed gonads bouncing away an inch from their face.

I did not travel on the train to London to picture what a flabby man's balls look like outside of their Lycra hellhole. This was not the deal when I paid my hard cash. My ticket does not say 'Brighton to London, all terminals with saggy balls'. It just says 'Brighton to London, all terminals.' 'It's great for the environment,' I hear them chirp. Not my environment. Great for my environment is a nice ambient temperature, a pleasant view, a comfortable seat and relative quiet. Maybe even a cheeky bottle of pop and some crisps. Call me conservative, but a great environment is not two sweaty skin plums an inch from my face.

Don't throw glasses around in a bar to impress punters

Of course, Tom Cruise is partly to blame for this. At the arse end of the 1980s, the film *Cocktail* featured a couple of self-obsessed dopes whose ability to juggle bottles behind a bar allowed them to bed Gina Gershon. This was a powerful message for a generation of idiots who thought that they too might get to bed Kelly Lynch were they able to keep bottles of beer in the air. It led to the development of the 'discipline' that is 'flair bartending' (bartenders entertaining punters with the manipulation of bar tools and bottles). This is also known as 'extreme bartending', a pastime whose exotic power is matched only by 'extreme TV watching' or 'extreme groin scratching'.

Here's the truth. If you throw bottles up and down while working behind a bar you won't bed Kelly Lynch. You won't even bed someone who looks like Kelly Lynch. You'll just break a lot of bottles.

Don't obsess about parking your car right outside your house

Most streets up and down the UK will have a curtain twitcher waiting patiently to make their move and relocate their car to their favourite spot. And you have to wonder how they always seem able to come out and move their car at the precise moment that a space becomes available. I think I might have figured it out. Picture the scene. It's 9.30 p.m. and it's pitch black. The blinds are down, the lights are lowered and our man sits on his knees in stakeout mode, a little tin of army rations next to him and a Swiss army knife (complete with comb) hanging from his trousers. His face is flecked with camouflage cream and a pile of *Beanos* and Dutch-strength skin mags lie at the base of the window. He peers through the blinds at the parking status of the street at regular intervals, perhaps varying the time between peeps lest someone else, equally paranoid, be monitoring his activity. He knows that he can't give those bastards an inch.

And then it happens. The klaxons sound, the alarm light turns neon red. Someone is leaving their house. His pulse flies to 200 bpm. He feels his hands tighten on his car keys (also attached to his belt). 'Come on, you little fucker, make my day,' he whispers and his Clint-isms betray the menace in his voice. False alarm, they are just getting something from their car. But it's too late; he has left his front door and stepped over the Rubicon. He's in full view of his competitors and suddenly he feels as naked as one of those animals in the special Scandinavian magazines he buys. Now he has to play it cool. He tells himself not to worry. He berates himself for both his haste and his unprofessional sense of panic. He is better than this. He moves like a viper to contingency plan B. He goes to check his tyre pressure, a cover for prying competitors who might wonder why he is out at this hour. But he checks them with his hands. Not great, he knows, but when in trouble you have to use the tools at your disposal. A million violent thoughts flood his head as he recovers his calm for the journey back to his front door. He knows the bastards can see him, he knows they are laughing at him, but he's got to keep his head held high and make it to the door. Not turn round, not give them the pleasure. He wants to let their tyres down, run over their cars with those big trucks with wheels the size of houses. He wants to set fire to their cars and make the owners watch. He tries to choke back the emotion, the rage and the confusion on the journey back. Now or never. He edges to the door. He can feel the draught of a million curtains twitching as they mock his error. He closes his front door and slides down it in a flood of tears, wailing with a mix of relief, anger and a curious semi-sexual excitement which even he has never quite understood. His time will come.

How do I recognize him?

OK, so you have just moved in, how are you going to recognize him in your street? You will know him because:

A) He almost always has a beard. Not big and fluffy, zoologist-style, but short and well-trimmed. Think Peter Sutcliffe or Jeremy Beadle.

B) He has had a beard since the age of three. If married, his wife will always have wondered why they don't have any family photos of her husband as a child but there is always a remarkably young-looking dwarf uncle hanging around in those that do exist.

C) He wears those strange clip-on shade things that people can hang on the bridge of their glasses and flip up. Indeed, he is the sole market for these sartorial travesties. Not a day goes by that he doesn't marvel at the rest of the world's idiocy for failing to notice just how user-friendly and functional these things are.

D) He carries a briefcase with nothing in it. The reason for this is that he likes being the only one who knows it's empty.

E) He will only talk to his children about cars, the weather and the limitations of their friends' parents as human beings. Were you to listen blindfolded to his discussion with his children, you would swear that he was talking to middle-aged men, such is the level of assumed knowledge.

F) His children think he is odd.

G) They are right.

A small selection of wives, girlfriends and children all over the western world are tonight eating alone as a strange little man is on his knees, fifteen yards from the dinner table, peeking through the Venetian blinds at the 'action' on the street.

Don't be a gadget bore

Like all members of a self-professed elite, men who love gadgets are smug bores. They don't love gadgets for any intrinsic value they might have, they love them because it allows them to have something that other people don't have. The gadget-lover thrives on the ultimate logic of the playground; they are the kid who can't wait to get to school to show his friends the toy/trainers etc. that they don't have yet. And this desperate desire to elevate themselves in front of others doesn't stop at gadgets. Oh no. They are the kind of men who wait with baited breath for people to make mistakes so that they can pounce on the error with a barely concealed, almost-sexual excitement. The kind of men who over-pronounce the names of foreign dishes and cities to show you how much more cosmopolitan and educated they are than you. Men who don't learn to broaden their minds but for the gratification of knowing that they know more than other people. They are the kind of men who correct other men for using terms like 'shag' and 'screw' and implore them to use terms like 'make love'. Not because they have a problem with the objectification of women but because they can make other men feel ignorant. And they like gadgets.

Don't walk without swinging your arms

If you are a man who doesn't swing his arms when he walks then you are considerably closer in lineage to our monkey ancestors than men who do swing their arms when they walk. Controversial, I know, but hear me out. There is hard biophysics behind this seemingly preposterous assertion. You see, when a person walks at a medium to brisk pace, they tend to swing their upper limbs in a contralateral fashion with the lower limbs. What that means is that their left foot and right hand move together and vice versa. Many experts believe that such a movement is necessary for balance in a species that spends one hundred per cent of its time walking on two legs. And less so for primates that don't.

Upright walking, or bipedalism, has long been considered a defining feature of humans. Now I am not saying these guys are not human *per se* (although in the interests of keeping an open mind it would be remiss of me to rule this out entirely), just that they are a little less human than the rest of us. In my completely unconsidered opinion, the degree of primate thinking in these men is that little bit greater than it is in the rest of us and I believe that this constitutes a concern. I am not saying that you are going to find these men hiding up trees and playing with each other's arseholes (although, again, it would not be fair to rule it out). I *am* saying that they are a bit more monkey than the rest of us and that this might not be a great thing, as monkeys are less intelligent, more feral and a bit more savage than your average human.

Don't like *Dirty Dancing*

Picture the scene. You go on holiday with your family and your seventeen-year-old daughter is roughly romanced by a moody, aggressive, deeply angry man of thirty-five (that's right, thirty-five), a man who makes screwing holiday-makers an art form. Call me old-fashioned, but I wouldn't like it either. She was seventeen for God's sake. And yet the dad is portrayed as a conservative, controlling father from an extinct generation standing in the way of his daughter's sexual awakening. No, he was trying to stop a border-line arrestable, taciturn brute from taking advantage of his daughter to the tune of 'I've had the time of my life'. 'Nobody puts baby in a corner'? No, they just take her to their room and fuck her instead.

Don't be a James Bond fantasist (don't fall into a tuxedo at the drop of a hat)

At university I encountered a phenomenon that I have always struggled get to grips with, something that I never quite understood and that I suspect my peers in the outside world – who had chosen to contribute more to their country than alcoholism, VD and unstinting support for the Che Guevara T-shirt market – weren't having to deal with. This something was the desire to dress up in a tuxedo at any given opportunity. Just how wedded a subculture of male undergraduates were to this particular look took me aback. I remember seeing one lad physically panting with excitement when he was made aware of another opportunity to get into black tie. I thought he was either going to ejaculate or have a stroke and, although I didn't know which, I knew that I didn't want to be around to find out. But what was the allure that had so shaken this lad's autonomic nervous system? And why did the evenings of the most-excited tuxedo wearers always seem to come to a tragically early denouement?

Then it dawned on me. Like Archimedes in the bath, I was struck by a revelation, a revelation that eschewed lazy accounts of sartorial elegance and maturity. This was all Sean Connery's fault. Well, Ian Fleming and Sean Connery's fault to be more precise. They were almost single-handedly responsible for associating the romance, action and excitement of being an international secret agent with the glamour and sophistication of wearing a tuxedo. And sophistication is key. It is very easy to be attracted to a man who literally knows everything. Bond was an expert in wine, languages, geography, culture, weapons, martial arts and technology. You name it, he had mastered it. Of course you were going to want to be like him. But the reality is that, in order to obtain such polymath expertise, he would have to be a bookish nerd who had not seen the light of day for twenty-five years. They would send this phenomenally knowledgeable, bilingual, killing machine out to foil the plans of the greatest criminal masterminds and he would be waylaid by the first comic-book convention he stumbled upon, poring over old issues of *Spiderman* while the earth blew to pieces.

Anyway, I digress. Generations of boys grew up wanting to be James Bond. Of course they did, why wouldn't they? The problem was that some, a select group, didn't see the 'actually it's no longer cool to want to be Bond' signposts at fourteen or fifteen. At about this age most guys start to have a few questions about Bond, questions that move him from the 'role model' category to the 'really like Bond films but maybe don't want to be Bond anymore' category.

Examples of things that make you begin to reappraise Bond at that age

- International diplomacy from democratically elected officials is a (marginally) more effective way to foil international terrorism than an armed sociopath whose appetite for rough sex would leave an imaginary Charlie Sheen/Prince hybrid languishing in the shade.
- Why would Richard Kiel's 'Jaws' be a cannibal or kill with his teeth just because they were metal? He was as capable of using a gun as the next man.
- You have to go to incredible lengths to construct a freak scenario that justifies the British taxpayer's money being spent on the design and production of an amphibious car.
- Not even if the Galores were crack-addled aliens in the middle of psychosis would they have thought Pussy was a good name for their daughter.
- By *A View to a Kill* Roger Moore was 103.
- Bond was generally an arsehole.

So, please guys, let's ditch the tuxedos, the Connery impressions ('Mish Moneypenny etc.) and the misquotes from *Goldfinger*. It's over.

Don't be an animal apologist

Let me tell you a little story about monkeys. In preparing for a lecture to a group of undergraduates I came upon a story written by a respected prima- tologist. This lady described an event that happened during a piece of research on a group of monkeys. Apparently a group of five monkeys from one monkey tribe decided to go after a single monkey from another monkey tribe. This monkey had committed the cardinal crime of hanging around their patch. Not unlike any nasty little skirmish you'd find in any dilapidated UK town centre on a Saturday night, they jumped the poor little bastard. Now here's the worrying part. Three monkeys held this other monkey down while two of their friends kicked and punched him. They beat this little thing to a pulp. To a pulp. Can you believe that? They held him down. I don't know if it's fair or whether it even makes sense to call a monkey a coward, but these little beasts were just that. Apparently, after failing to report the crime to the monkey police on the grounds that it was just a few mates having a few drinks too many (OK I made that bit up), the victim monkey wandered around in a daze for a couple of days and then died (true). The primatologist didn't provide any information on what the aggressor monkeys were wearing but I like to think that they were wearing hoodies and smoking fags and made their getaways on monkey motorbikes while whooping and firing their guns indiscriminately into the air.

So all those idealists who are so keen to impute positive human values onto hairy beasts can think again. Monkeys are most certainly not gentle. If they do this, who knows what else they do? Perhaps in years to come we will hear a primatologist's report on monkeys who push younger monkeys onto hard drugs through selling them soft drugs and gradually using monkey peer- pressure to move them onto skag. Or maybe they'll spot monkeys wearing leopard-skin suits and gold-rimmed platforms and a feather in their hats pimping out some local girl monkeys who have fallen on hard times but need the cash to put their kids through monkey school. Watch this space.

I should note at this juncture that qualified primatologists are not the only people who have noticed this phenomenon. I have also observed monkey behaviour that fails to support this notion of monkeys as generous, benevolent creatures whose only wish is to take part in 5 k runs for children's cancer hospices. In Singapore Zoo I saw a monkey slap another monkey in the face and run away. And it wasn't just a normal slap, it was a bitch slap. Now even in the monkey world the bitch slap has to be a pretty humiliating event and the monkey who had been slapped looked utterly bereft. The perpetrator could have punched him, but he chose to publicly bitch slap him. There, animal lovers, do you love our simian friends quite so much now? Wonder if Dian Fossey would have spent eternity in a wet jungle if she knew these little critters were acting like angry rap stars.

Don't be a pushy daddy

I have a confession to make: I don't like pushy fathers. Why do I find them so contemptible? Well, I think that the heart-warming case of seven-year-old Braxton Bilbrey helps here. A few years ago little Braxton braved cold and shark-infested waters to swim from Alcatraz Island to the San Francisco shore, a feat no inmate managed during its time as an active penitentiary. Braxton's coach, Joe Zemaitis, noted with obvious pride that only 1 in 10 million boys his age could have managed the 1.4 mile swim in choppy waters. Now I'm not going to start to question coach Zemaitis' understanding of the rudimentaries of probability theory. Let's just leave it by saying that he clearly pulled this number out of his arse. I will, however, focus on WHETHER A SEVEN-YEAR-OLD CHILD SHOULD HAVE A COACH TO SWIM ACROSS COLD, SHARK-INFESTED WATERS!!!

Please someone, for the love of God, tell me where the local social services were? Why does a seven-year-old child have a coach to do something that the majority of adults would struggle with or struggle to even care about? Apparently, with little Braxton, 'It's all coming from him; it's more a ques-

tion, not of pushing him too hard, but of having to hold him back.' And this is the ever-popular refrain from defensive pushy daddies when questioned on their manic desire to live vicariously through the achievements of their children: 'It's what they want.' Of course it is. These fathers are little more than hapless vessels driven to supporting these miniature forces of nature and their curious desire to inflict punishment on themselves. I can imagine the conversation at the breakfast table:

'Daddy, could you pass the toast, please?'
'Sure, here it is, son.'
'Daddy, can you take me to school today?'
'Sure, son, we'll leave in ten minutes.'
'Also, would it be OK if I stayed over at Tom's house this weekend?'
'Well, sure, as long as it's OK with Tom's parents.'
'Also Dad, would you mind hiring me a coach to break the record for swimming to Alcatraz and back?'

Of course it came from him. Just as I'm sure that benign and loving fathers around the world are being approached with requests such as, 'Daddy, rather than sleeping in this morning would you mind if I got up at 4.30 a.m. to do two hours of swimming training before school and then go again afterwards for two hours? I'm just not falling asleep enough in class at the moment.' Or maybe they're being asked, 'Daddy, can I be taught three hours of piano every day by a very angry woman so that I can be brought out of bed on Saturday night to show your dinner party circuit how adept I am at Pachelbel's *Canon in D*? Also, if I get one note wrong, can you angrily force me to play the whole thing again and apologize to your guests on my behalf?' Or perhaps further still, 'Dad, I know it sounds strange, but would you mind if I signed up for private after-school Latin classes? It's just that I'm worried that I'm falling behind on my ability to speak languages that nobody else speaks.' Not likely.

What you actually need for pushy fathers is a self-delusion translator. A device that allows them to feed in their apparently benign desires, beliefs and intentions for their children and have the realities reflected back to them. Now, granted, I haven't yet put the final touches on the electro-magnetics of such a device, so I'm constrained here to explaining how it might work in principle. The pushy daddy can feed in the following idea for their child:

'Honey, I really think that Timmy should enter the local chess competition. With his brain he will be truly exceptional. I think he has an excellent chance of winning.'
'Actually, that's a good idea, love. And what's more, I think it will really challenge him and allow him to move ahead at a rate that will maximize his potential. It's so important we do everything we can for him at this age.'

A quick flick into my self-delusion translator and this comes out as:

'Honey, would it be OK to set little Timmy up for a lifetime of bullying?'
'I don't know darling, will it allow you the ephemeral thrill of momentarily increasing your self-worth and social standing among your friends?'

'Kind of. A bit anyway.'

'Then hell, let's do it, fill your boots.'

'Great! Then let's get him entered in one of those child chess competitions that are renowned for producing well-adjusted and happy kids. Certainly little Timmy won't take an absolute beasting from a couple of brutes who don't care much for the intricacies of the Sicilian defence.'

The bottom line is that we get the fact that you, the father, were very average and didn't achieve much in your childhood. We also get the fact that your adulthood probably hasn't been a continuous battle to fend off professional and personal plaudits either. But please, try not to wear these failings as a badge through the hounding of your poor, unfortunate child.

Don't do competition bodybuilding

Picture the scene: it's the planet Zarg, millions of light years from earth. One clever Zargian has managed to design a spaceship to go and look at other intergalactic populations to try to find new and exciting ways in which to improve the Zarg race. After many years of interplanetary travel they report back to their leader on all the wonderful, interesting and useful things they have seen:

'And tell me, intrepid travellers, was there anything you came across on your travels that vexed you?'

'Well, actually boss, there was one thing.'

'Please my child, do go on.'

'Weeeeell. We came across a group of Earthlings; they were mostly men, but some women too. Their lives consisted of spending all of their time in sweaty rooms, religiously working specific muscle groups. Now and again they took steroids or natural supplements to become bigger, shaved their bodies of hair, spent hours under a sun lamp and regularly smothered themselves in oil. They then starved themselves for days on end and stood on a stage and flexed furiously to judges while pretending to smile. And their balls looked really small.'

'Very interesting. And why did they do this?'

'Well, nobody really seemed to know.'

Don't be seen dead on a skateboard

A good friend of mine has a theory that he calls his *Logan's Run* music theory (after the film). He states that no modern musician has ever done anything of worth after their thirtieth birthday. Moreover, he would stop anyone from recording music after their thirtieth birthday. The advantages, such as the cancellation of all those Paul McCartney and David Bowie/Tin Machine missteps, are hopefully clear for all. He argues, convincingly, that after that age people simply lose their creative, artistic spark – the hunger and energy

that once allowed them to create something unique, electric, and exciting. And it's this theory that I will apply to adult men who play on skateboards. They are the skateboarding equivalent of REM post Bill Berry: vapid, bloated has-beens frantically trying to recreate something that died a long time ago. For the skateboard represents the dying embers of their youth, a time of vigour and excitement, relevance and rebellion, when the world was a place full of potential glory rather than a nine to five drudge where the only excitement is trying to figure out how to extract their balls from the vice-like grip of their boss. It makes perfect sense that an adult male would want a skateboard to recreate a sense of nostalgic vim and relevance. But it doesn't work. Unless you are a master in the art of self-deception, you will sooner or later come to realize that a) you are an old, fat bloke on a skateboard and b) old and fat on a skateboard looks even older and fatter than normal. Let it go, it's over.

Don't wear combat trousers unless you're a soldier

Combat trousers tend to be worn by the armed forces, particularly soldiers in arenas of conflict around the world. They are necessary in order to help these soldiers evade detection by allowing them to blend into their environment. There is, however, a further use of combat trousers. They are also worn by a select minority of men in the UK who use these trousers in their own – very different, but equally taxing – battle: to lose their virginities. And in this battle jeans, tracksuit trousers, suit trousers and corduroy simply will not suffice.

Adult men who wear combat trousers tend to have a number of rare abilities which, when taken together, constitute a formidable skill-set. Firstly, they tend to be very, very good at computer games, particularly computer games that involve shooting the characters of other combat-trouser-wearing men around the world, who are also enduring a sustained tour of duty in the battle to lose their virginities. They will be experts at showing local children their

penknife collections and telling them grandiose stories about themselves that aren't true. For instance, I was cleaning my car one day when, in one gloriously ostentatious ten-minute period, I had the pleasure of hearing our local combat-trouser-wearing man-child tell a couple of local children that he a) had been a film stuntman, but didn't like to talk about it since 'the accident' (convenient), b) could do more press-ups than Ross Kemp from

EastEnders (technically not impossible) and c) had three girlfriends on the go because he liked to keep them keen (definitely impossible). A pretty impressive list of achievements for a man who looked for all the world as if Danny DeVito had convinced Steve Buscemi to lend him his head. These men form solid platonic friendships with local children until asked not to by said children's parents. Were they to go on *Mastermind*, John Humphries would be a little taken aback by their outstanding performance on their specialist subject of extreme Dutch pornography, 1980–2011. Finally, a considerable number of them will adorn their gardens proudly with a skull and crossbones flag. Should anyone in the local area not have already realized, this flag will reinforce the understanding that this man is more likely than not to have had to visit A&E after getting drunk and forcefully romancing his Dyson. Moreover, these guys are usually pretty adept at that trick from the film *Aliens*, where you lay your hand on a table and quickly stab a dagger across the gaps between your fingers. Until they make a mistake and nick a finger, at which point they'll say that it didn't even hurt. Finally, it's likely that they will commonly be heard expressing the idiosyncratic opinion that all of the problems of the world could be solved by Hugh Hefner (probably in tandem with Jason Statham).

There is no doubt in my mind that this would be quite a skill-set in a world where the sole purpose of an adult man was to electrify impressionable youngsters. Sadly though, things are a little trickier in reality. In our world, you need to do more than be good at pretending that your air rifle is a real gun while wearing an Iron Maiden T-shirt.

Don't wear red trousers

Just don't.

Don't wear tight tops if you start to develop moobs

I myself am no stranger to the agony of the man boob or 'moob'. Once, when I was a PhD student, I was teaching statistics to a class of undergraduates. As I was explaining the joys of a mixed analysis of variance to a group of about fifty increasingly suicidal students, I noticed them momentarily stop fashioning their nooses and taking a renewed interest in me. Whereas I obviously took this to be my teaching breakthrough moment à la Robin Williams in *Dead Poets' Society*, it eventually became obvious that the students were not looking at the whiteboard, nor were they actually looking at my face. At the time I had (actually, I still have) a dreadful tendency to retain clothes that even the most destitute hobo would slap you for offering him, and that day I was wearing a very old T-shirt. What I didn't realize was that a) it had a small hole on the left of my chest and, more critically, b) my left man-boob had gravitated across in such a fashion that a chubby nipple had popped its head out and was waving hello to my newly invigorated students. Red-faced and speechless, I pulled my T-shirt down, I tucked it in, I pulled it across, I folded my arms, I lifted my shoulders – I literally tried everything, but nothing could stop this naughty disco tit, who was clearly hell-bent on having his moment in the sun. My ability to convey the finer points of said analysis took a nosedive so I set them an exercise to work on, and subsequently tried to figure out which of my students thought I was a pervert and which of them thought I was a moron. As it happens I had it at about 80:20 for pervert.

There are a number of options open to men with moobs and they don't have to involve publicly exposing yourself. First of all, however, you have to know that you have man-boobs and it's not altogether easy to know at exactly what point your previously flat chest died and became reincarnated as a pair of floppy disco tits. Don't worry though, I've included a couple of tests below for those out there who are at the point of transition:

Stage one: Beat your chest with a closed fist. Does it make a meaningful noise? If so, continue to laugh at the older men at work who look like they suckle pigs. If your closed fist momentarily disappears from view and you have to pull it out using your other hand, move to stage two.

Stage two: Spend some time with a friend/family member who is breast-feeding a young child. Ask to hold the child and wait patiently to see if anyone makes a joke about you being able to breastfeed them. You're in a room with nice people who wouldn't make a joke like that? No problem. Make the joke yourself and notice how many people have a look of relief on their face that suggests that you said what everyone was thinking. If it's over half the people in the room, move to stage three.

Stage three: Sit down with a trusted male friend and ask them whether they would have a crack at you in a nightclub if they could only see you from your chest to the bottom of your neck. If the answer is yes, move to stage four.

Stage four: It's over and you know it.

Assuming that you are going to continue to avoid the gym or a meaningful diet then you have three options if you want to try to hide your moobs. Option one is a short term measure and involves hitching your shoulders up a little higher than normal. This works by stretching the man boob out and, in some cases, making it temporarily disappear altogether. The problem with this is that you then look like somebody has stolen your neck when you weren't looking, so you have to balance looking mooby against looking neck-less. Moreover, if your moobs are particularly voluminous you might end up looking neck-less *and* mooby, so this needs careful thought. Now option two isn't really an option at all. The men who choose option two seem to be under the misapprehension that tight tops get rid of moobs. And not just any tight tops. For some reason, these men seem particularly drawn toward sleeve-less, hooded tops so snug that they require the wearer to jump off their wardrobe head first to get into them. Why it should be that sleeveless, hooded tops are *de rigueur* clothing for the disco-titted male, I don't really know. Perhaps, like the telegram that arrives at your door should you be unfortunate enough to reach a hundred years old, the Queen also takes an active interest in chubby males when their he-knockers have reached a critical size. One has to assume that these men are operating under the same principle as the Victorian women who pretended to be men by tightly wrapping their breasts to their bodies. The problem is that tight clothing alone doesn't actually achieve this effect. Such men are correct in their basic logic that tight clothes will flatten the moob, but only insofar as the wearer comes to look like the first adult man who has figured out how to breastfeed a family of ten children. Instead of just sporting the indignity of moobs, they have created the ultimate physical indignity of saggy moobs. This is not good. Option three? If you want to avoid rocking up at your local nightclub looking as though you thought it was a fancy dress night with a porky simpleton theme, there really is only one option. Speaking as one who knows, thick fabrics and loose shirts are probably your best bet for damage limitation.

Don't go topless in town centres

There is absolutely nothing wrong with walking around a busy town centre on a Saturday bare-chested as long as you are content with your fellow shoppers assuming the following about you:

- You're proud of finally conquering the noble art of breathing and walking at the same time and you want to show as many people as possible.
- There is nothing you love more than hitting people in the face.
- And making people feel nervous about being hit in the face. That's nice too.
- There's nothing you would like more than for someone to brush against you.
- Or look at you funny. Because then you could hit them in the face.
- You believed in Santa until the age of thirteen. When you found out he wasn't real you wanted to do someone.
- You can never understand why Bonnie Tyler's 'Holding Out for a Hero' doesn't accompany your every move.
- You wear tracksuit trousers to weddings.
- You want to show other people that you have muscles. Since other people are wearing their clothes you have assumed that they must not have muscles like you have. That must mean they won't be as good at hitting people in the face as you are.
- Your tried and tested method of expressing interest in a member of the opposite sex is to call them a fucking slag and beat them at an arm-wrestle.
- Out of all your mates, you're the best at sniffing glue.
- You once counted to seventeen, although you're not sure if you did it right.

Otherwise you should always keep your top on.

Don't make paintball a hobby

Stag nights have changed in recent years. The age-old tried and tested formula of a night at the local pub trying to pretend that fourteen pints don't touch the sides has slowly morphed into long weekends in Prague where skydiving, go-karting and hot-air ballooning are all to be got out of the way before lunch on the first day. One activity that has become synonymous with the modern stag do is paintball. Paintball, for the uninitiated, is the modern equivalent of being in the Territorial Army. You are given paint pellets and a gun and then released into a wooded area where you are repeatedly shot in the balls and arse while trying to figure out how to stop being blinded by your steamed-up goggles. You do this for around an hour under the pretence of finding a flag. Once you have mastered this, you use this newfound confidence to do a few special forces rolls on the ground before more shots on your balls and arse make you think better of it. You then wait quietly behind a bush until it's all finished and then go and get leathered in the pub and make up stories about how close you got to the flag and how it took fourteen

shots to bring you down. So far, so good. Until, of course, the semi-professional paintballers turn up and ruin it for everyone. These are men who go to paintball every weekend (and sometimes more) with the express purpose of taking advantage of newbie stag-party participants. They know all the right places to hide, have superior clothing and weaponry and are utterly enthralled by the activity of repeatedly firing paint into the groins and faces of naive newcomers just trying to have a bit of fun with their friends. Make no mistake, these men are low. The scale of the mismatch forces one into the assumption that such men obtain a similarly electric sense of achievement from hiding the walking canes of frail and partially blind pensioners and beating newborns at Connect Four. It is not unusual for such men to wear bandannas, just in case their regular attendance at paintball was not a sufficient marker of their long and wearying histories of premature ejaculation.

I would argue, however, that there is little real glory in giving a monumental paintball hiding to a couple of stag parties if afterwards you go home and argue with your mum about how unfair it is that you can't wear your Superman costume when you watch *Superman*.

Don't audibly strain in a public toilet cubicle

It is one of the great frustrations of my life that the person charged with the historic task of designing public-toilet cubicles was armed with an IQ that precluded them from farting without laughing. Someone, somewhere thought that a satisfactory barrier between cubicles in a public toilet constituted a thin piece of wood with a gap at the bottom and the top. That person made the decision that a comfortable public-toilet experience required only that you didn't see the person next to you. This level of public toilet privacy seems to be one of the many substandard features of modern living that we seem to have accepted in the western world, like the presence of Lego-like chairs on long-haul flights, cancelled trains and Mick Hucknall. However, the presence of a few unwritten rules in public toilets helps to reduce the potential problems of these cubicles. For instance, it's considered poor form to throw the contents of your cubicle over the side and mimic the noise of bombs exploding as these land on your neighbour, or to slip your puppetted hands under toilet-cubicle walls and treat your neighbour to an impromptu reworking of the Karma Sutra. Another rule is that you don't vocalize your suffering if you are engaged in a battle with an entity that is tearing its way through your bowels. Taking a dump has become a curiously public affair, but there is no need to turn it into a performance. Now I'm as much of a realist as the next person. I get that you are going to hear evacuation noises that you're not going to want to request for your iPod and I get that you are going to experience smells that make you want to Taser your neighbour on the ankle. But audible straining? This I simply can't accept. This I have experienced on numerous occasions when I simply went in for a piss only to find myself savagely yanked into another man's personal anal hell.

One particularly extreme example stands out. Only recently I went in to use the public toilet at work. I needed to empty my bowels, so I did my usual checks of the four cubicles to see if I was on my own. One cubicle was busy and normally this would be an invitation to return at a later date, but my bowels were telling me in no uncertain terms that walking away could land me in code-red territory. So I did my usual inspections. Toilet paper? Check. Seat that's not addled with (much) fresh piss? Check. Pan that doesn't look like it could potentially house a razor-toothed bog creature that could pounce and feast on my dangling genitals? Check. Ish. I pulled down my trousers in such a way that they didn't become saturated with the floor piss and went about my own business.

What subsequently transpired should not happen to anybody. My anonymous companion started to whimper. Moreover, it was the whimper of a man whose rectum was being asked to do a job that it clearly hadn't signed up for. He didn't just sound pained but genuinely scared, like he was passing something that he figured might have the capability of chasing him out of the toilet. Slowly the whimper grew to a groan and then to a full howl as he made noises I'd only previously heard in a maternity suite. His suffering climaxed with an audible whine of, 'Oh don't, oh Christ'. That's right, he was actually talking to this thing, trying to reason with it, like it could be reasoned with. Now it is my contention that I shouldn't have had to listen to that, to the suffering of a man forced into the altogether hopeless act of pleading with his own faeces to take it easy on his rectum. Is it right that I should be exposed to the supremely private act of a man forced to become a hostage negotiator for his own butthole? There are so many indignities that can be visited upon modern humans but surely among the most atrocious is being forced to listen to a man publicly reason with his own rectum. I only wanted to use the toilet. High-minded critics have suggested that self-consciousness is the key attribute that separates humans from our primate cousins. I only wish that not having to hear another man defecating was another.